LUCKY ENOUGH

A Year of a Dad's Daily Notes of Encouragement
and Life Lessons to his Daughter

CHRIS YANDLE

PAGE PUBLISHING, INC.
New York, NY

First originally published by Page Publishing, Inc. 2018

ISBN 978-1-64350-735-4 (Paperback)
ISBN 978-1-64350-736-1 (Digital)

Printed in the United States of America

For Addison

We live in a data-rich age,
but we are a wisdom-deficit society.

#DadLunchNotes

ACKNOWLEDGMENT

Thank you to those who donated money to help make this dream become a reality. I never thought there would be people interested in donating money for a book I wanted to write. Alas, there were more than sixty of you who believed in me when I didn't believe in myself. Thank you.

To my wife, who supported this idea from the start, and for all the quotes you send to me, thank you! I love you, Ashleigh.

Perhaps most importantly, to my daughter, Addison. Thank you for allowing me to share what I write with the masses. I hope you will always cherish this book. I love you, pumpkin.

INTRODUCTION

Chris, I'm pregnant.

These are both the happiest and scariest words a man can hear his wife, girlfriend, or significant other utter. I was paralyzed with the same level of fear and excitement as my wife told me. Did I mention that she told me over the phone while I was on a business trip?

From the moment my wife, Ashleigh, broke the news, I was hoping—nay, praying—for a little girl. For whatever reason, I thought the storybook example of fatherhood was to be a dad to a little girl. Maybe it was the way my older sister (unhealthily) worshipped our dad or how my wife looked at hers, but I wanted a girl. I was a nervous wreck for the next eight months—from our doctor's appointments to figuring out how I was going to afford a kid to realizing, "Holy ——, I'm going to be a father. To an actual human life. I can't even manage to wash clothes properly."

Those eight months were the most confusing of my life. And until the ensuing eight months when I'm staring at the formula section of our local H-E-B at 2:00 a.m.

I desperately wanted a little girl. And a little girl I got. Weighing in at a paltry six pounds, fourteen ounces, a long-legged, scrawny, crying bundle of jaundice joy emerged from my wife's belly at 7:30 a.m. on Thursday, July 3, 2008.

I was instantly smitten by her.

Sure, she had no idea who the hell I was or the journey we were about to embark, but she was mine.

There aren't many memories I vividly recall, but I do remember this: the nurse handed her over and said, "Here you go, Dad."

"What ... what do I do?" I asked nervously.

The nurse chuckled. "Well, this is your daughter. You can walk her to the room. Mom will be there shortly."

Sleeping now, she and I walked down the hall to our room where the grandparents were waiting. This was reality now.

Some thirty-six hours later, I was leaving my wife and now one-day-old infant at the hospital as I was driving a Penske truck full of our possessions to our new home four hundred miles away in Texas for a new job I started three days later. As you can presumably already tell, I'm a planner … and a tad bit crazy. More planner than crazy, I hope.

These last ten years have been one helluva journey. Every day, I do my best not to screw up, knowing that all of us as parents are nowhere near perfect and that we all make mistakes. In reality, my ultimate goal is to raise a respectable young woman—and to not have to send her to therapy until high school.

* * * * *

Why do I write her notes? Why now?

The first part is easier to answer first: I *write* because it's easy for me.

Growing up, I was a painfully shy kid. When I got older, I realized I was really a stone-cold introvert. It was hard for me to verbalize my feelings. I didn't think anyone wanted to hear them, so I kept them to myself. With each passing year, writing came more and more naturally to me. Speaking in front of my peers was painful, but writing was pain-free. Either way, my feelings and thoughts were being shared, but for whatever reason, writing them on paper was easier for me.

When I got to high school, I was a champ at writing notes to girls. But alas, the rejection still came in written form. Funny, it was easier to bear reading the words "friend zone" rather than hearing them aloud. As I've watched my little girl grow up, I've come to realize, my wife gave birth to Chris 2.0.

She is almost my mirror image, so I know how hard it can be to express yourself verbally, and I wanted the two of us to have something that no one else has.

Why *now*?

In March 2016, I was informed that I was not being retained by my employer and that my contract would expire in three months. Fired. Let go. Contract not renewed. Whatever you called it, I was out of a job. I will be the first to admit—although begrudgingly—

that I was not a basket of rainbows and puppy dogs before I lost my job or after. I wasn't the dad I needed to be. My depression was at an all-time low. I was a "dead man walking" every day at a job that didn't want me, and I wasn't mentally present at home.

I had checked out.

When I walked out of my office for the last time, I was broken. I didn't believe I was a good father figure. With all these thoughts swirling in my head, my wife and I decided it would be best for all of us to pack up and move back home to south Louisiana. It was time.

While I wasn't in the right frame of mind to offer any type of life advice to my two kids, they (and my wife too) were the only things that kept me sane and pushed me to get up each morning. As my daughter transitioned to her third school in four years, I watched in amazement at her resiliency at such a young age, but I know there were obstacles that lay ahead of us.

Toward the end of her third-grade year, we were faced with another reality—Addison would be starting her *fourth* school in five years. This was nothing like we had planned. We didn't think we'd take the path we did, but here we were. My nine-year-old daughter was entering—*gulp!*—middle school as a fourth grader. Since my wife was once a girl, she knew that middle school could be awful for girls. Fourth grade is a pivotal time in her development.

And besides, she's about to enter the "I hate you, Dad!" part of her life, so I wanted to instill as many lessons and ideas as I could and collect as many good memories as possible!

(JK on the "I hate you, Dad!" part, I hope.)

* * * * *

The next two hundred or so pages are filled with notes and messages I wrote to Addison during her fourth-grade school year. Some of them are things my dad told me at her age or while I was in college. Others are things I've learned personally along the way. You may notice that some days are missing—neither Addison nor Daddy had perfect school attendance this year.

Either way, I hope some of these messages can resonate with your own children or provide some affirmation on how life can be sometimes. One of things I added to this project was for you, the parent, to share with your significant other and use it as a tool with your kids.

I would love to hear how this book and this idea resonated with you.

Love,
Dad

DAY 1

August 14, 2017

Addy,

Be nice to others. Not everyone will look like you. Learn to spot the unique and special things in other people. You have the power to change someone's life!

Love,
Dad

Honest moment here: this was the third day of the new school year. I had noticed that Addison was unsure of her new school after the first two days, and I didn't know what I was doing as a dad. I was having an internal fight with myself: Do I write notes to my daughter to reinforce the good things in life? Do I give her advice? Will she understand what I'm saying? Will she think I'm a dork? All this was happening in the time it took me to make her lunch—two minutes.

You see all these cool Instagram dads doing these encouraging things for their kids. I think I'm funny, but my funny jokes are usually met with "You're not funny, Daddy." So that's out of the window, but I wanted her to know that I was paying attention to what she was experiencing.

The hardest person to be in the world now is a girl growing up. I wanted Addison to know I'd always be her biggest fan.

DAY 2

August 15, 2017

Addy,

Treat everyone like they are the most important person you'll ever meet.

Love,
Dad

In my career, this is one of the adages I always tried to follow. As a leader, I didn't always follow the words I spoke, and I lost my job because of it. We live in a "me society" where we only focus on ourselves. While it's healthy for us to have "me time," it is not, however, healthy to always be self-centric. Focusing on others and sharing ourselves with others can give us a healthier balance within our lives.

People who focus on others and are genuinely interested in the lives and values of other people tend to be happier. (I'm pretty sure that's a scientific fact.) Truth of the matter is, I want my kids to treat others with respect because I know not everyone is going to treat them with the respect they deserve.

If I get anything right as a parent, it's that I want my kids to live every day knowing that other people can add value to their lives.

DAY 3

August 16, 2017

Addy,

What you think of yourself is much more important than what others think of you.

Love,
Dad

I spent too much—and I still do—of my adolescent and adult life worrying about what others think about me. For whatever reason, I'm consumed by what faceless Twitter avatars say about me. I remember being a nine-year-old in fourth grade in a Catholic school. It sucked. That was almost thirty years ago, and I know middle school kids can be meaner and harsher critics in today's *InstaSnapFace* world.

I don't want my daughter to grow up with the same insecurities as me and her mom, Ashleigh, did. Years of therapy made strides to undo the damage, but the scars still remain.

I know it's easier said than done, but who cares what other people think of you? Unless you are one of my kids and the other people are your parents, then you should care because we love you. Don't waste your energy on people who can do nothing for you.

Oh! I need to write that saying down for later.

DAY 4

August 17, 2017

Addy,

Always give your best. In everything you do. I don't care if you don't win or if you don't always get good grades, as long as you gave it *your best*!

Love,
Dad

Throughout my time in school, I was jealous of my classmates who would get straight As, but they worked hard. They always gave their best. To them, Bs weren't their best. Looking back at my time in grade school, I was bored. I didn't devote many hours to studying. I took notes in class, but I didn't pay much attention. I'd get As and Bs with a few Cs sprinkled here and there.

I didn't give my best. I knew I wasn't giving my best every day. I was operating at 70 percent of my capability. When I'd get a D, I knew I had to pretend to give a damn, so I'd try a little bit more to inch up to a C+ or a B-.

In college, I repeated my bad habits, but those bad habits led to dean's list every semester of undergrad and grad school. I didn't learn, but I know one thing—I don't want my kids to make the same mistakes of not giving 100 percent (110 percent is cliché and not attainable).

DAY 5

August 18, 2017

Addy,

There are 86,400 seconds in a day. Take a few seconds to tell someone *thank you*.

Love,
Dad

I learned a tough lesson along the way: You don't get places on your own, and when you make it to the next stop on your journey, you need to thank those who helped get you there. During the early part of my career, I thought I climbed the mountain all by myself. No help, no guidance. All Chris, all glory.

<<insert record scratch>>

Yeah, that's not how life works. Needless to say, I was humbled—quickly. I now try to live a life of gratitude. I was raised to be a Southern gentleman, I think, so I make an effort to say "please," "yes, ma'am," "no, ma'am," and "thank you" every day. At the very least, my kids can be taught to tell people "thank you" because that appears to be a lost art among the younger generation.

I even make my kids handwrite thank-you notes to relatives before they can enjoy the fruits of their birthday and Christmas loot.

DAY 6

August 21, 2017

Addy,

Treat others the way you want to be treated. Be your sweet and funny self.

Love,
Dad

Jack! That's usually what Ashleigh and I hear on a semihourly basis in our house. Our lovely, beautiful nine-year-old daughter turned into a hormone-infused anger monster as she screams at her six-year-old brother who just wants to be with her. We constantly remind both of our kids that they should treat others the way they want to be treated.

Let's role-play for a minute.

Addison: *Jack!* Get. Out. Of. My. *Room!*

Jackson: Ad-dy, don' talk to me that way!

Dad: Addison, how would you feel if someone spoke to you like that?

Addison: (*Grumbling with her arms crossed.*) I wouldn't like it.

Jackson: It's okay, Ad-dy.

Dad: No, it's not because I know your sister wouldn't like it if you spoke to her that way.

Less than five minutes later.

Jack! (Ah, the joys of refereeing—er—parenting).

DAY 7

August 22, 2017

Addy,

A day without laughter is a day wasted. Laugh often!

Love,
Dad

I don't laugh enough. I mean, I make almost everyone I meet laugh because I'm a naturally funny person (insert laugh here). Somewhere over the years, I stopped laughing. That sounds weird, but it's true.

"You don't laugh enough" is what Ashleigh tells me almost daily, and she's right. I don't. I need to laugh more. As each day goes by, I start to notice that Addison is—*gasp!*—becoming my identical twin. While Ashleigh constantly reaffirms to me that being like me is a great thing, all I think about are my small eccentric idiosyncrasies that make me not so fun to be with at times. One of those idiosyncrasies is that lack of laughter.

Addison doesn't laugh enough. She doesn't even laugh at my jokes! While that might just be my humor being too advanced for a nine-year-old, it makes me worried. I want her to love life. I want her to be happy. I don't want her to take life too seriously like I did as a kid and as a teenager.

I'm still trying to undo all the knots that humor didn't undo decades ago.

DAY 8

August 23, 2017

Addy,

No one is keeping score of what you do as a kid. Have fun. Enjoy every day. Laugh. Play. Learn. But more importantly, have fun!

Love,
Dad

Addison doesn't like sports while Jackson thinks he's going to be the first five-sport professional athlete.

"No one is keeping score of what you do as a kid."

They're not. When I coached Jackson's basketball and soccer teams this season, the kids would ask me, "Coach, what's the score? Who's winning? How many points to do we have?"

I would always tell them, "No one is keeping score of what you do as a kid. Just have fun, guys."

To which my son would respond, "Daddy, that's not the score. It's …"

So much for trying to teach life lessons to a gaggle of five- and six-year-old boys.

Parents today are so infested with the pipe dream of their children playing sports and getting a full athletic scholarship to play whatever sport at a *big college U.* As someone who worked in college sports for a decade, I know that this type of thinking is toxic. Plus, if these are truly my kids, then I *know* they won't get an athletic scholarship because I have no athletic ability whatsoever.

So far, Jackson has proven that. He gives every sport every ounce of energy he's got, but he still runs like me—a refrigerator with legs.

No one's keeping score.

DAY 9

August 24, 2017

Addy,

Listen twice as much as you speak. Always listen
to what people have to say.

Good luck on your tests!

Love,
Dad

Sometimes we listen with the intent to respond, not the intent
to understand. I'm guilty of this at times. We live in a world of talk,
talk, talk, talk. No one listens anymore. Everyone wants to be heard.
That's not how conversation works.

We have two ears and one mouth. Naturally, we should listen
twice as much as we speak. However, oftentimes we speak twice
as much as we listen. That's where we get into trouble and where
miscommunication happens.

We want people to listen to what we have to say. We can fix this
pattern by listening to what others are saying, processing it, and then
responding to them. We're too busy trying to preserve our thoughts
and self-efficacy that we don't take the few seconds to digest what the
other person is saying.

When your child comes home and wants to talk, put down
your phone and listen to every single syllable he or she has to say.
Answer their questions. Don't talk over them.

Listen twice as much as you speak.

DAY 10

August 25, 2017

Addy,

Always stand up for what's right. Your voice is your power.

Love,
Dad

There's injustice all around us, but staying silent is just as bad—if not worse—than being the person committing the injustice. I want my kids to stand up for what's right. See something? Say something. It's as simple as that.

But there's a difference between standing up for what's right and being a tattletale. For better or worse, I've taught my kids that "snitches get stitches" if they tattle on people. I tell them this not because I'm in the mob or a street gang but for them to understand the difference between the two.

People that cheat and cut corners will get their comeuppance eventually. It may not be today, it may not be tomorrow, but it will come. Don't stand up for that. Stand up for those who are bullied.

Stand up when someone is prejudiced against another person.

Stand up when someone has been discriminated against.

Stand up for what's right.

Use your voice for good.

DAY 11

August 28, 2017

Addy,

No one is perfect, but cats are purrrr-fect. Cats don't worry about making mistakes. Be a cat!

Love,
Dad

To break up the string of seriousness, I decided to use my humor pen for good. Instead of a chuckle, I got a half smirk from my Addison, who then asked, "Why do you want me to be a cat?"
Sigh.

DAY 12

August 29, 2017

Addy,

Kindness costs $0. It's *free*. Everyone wants free stuff. Give them kindness!

Love,
Dad

Money's tight. We're always looking for free stuff. What's the best type of deposit you make to your bank account (besides, you know, money)?

Kindness.

Kindness is free. We aren't kind enough to one another. We're all too caught up in our own lives that instead of being a planet filled with seven billion people, we are seven billion individual planets bouncing around in a huge snow globe called Earth.

Make a kindness deposit in someone's bank account every day. As I tell my kids and later wrote to Addison, you could make someone's day or change their life with your kindness. Be there for others. Not only will it positively affect their life, but it will also positively affect your life too.

Kindness leads to gratitude, which—hopefully—leads to a thankful way of life.

DAY 13

August 30, 2017

Addy,

Don't ever let someone else determine your value.
You're always worth everything.

Love,
Dad

You'll see this once again toward the end of the school year, but this was the first time Ashleigh and I started noticing something different in Addison's demeanor. She wouldn't tell us what was going on because—you know—parents ruin *everything*. Ugh.

When I was nine, we didn't have the internet or social media. We didn't have the immense media and peer pressure that kids do today. Kids younger and younger are comparing themselves to celebrities on the covers of magazines. They are comparing each other's social media followers.

We're all measuring our quality of life and our value and what we perceive to be someone else's awesome quality of life or perceived higher value. Spoiler alert: We all have the same value. We're all worth the same thing.

No amount of filtered Instagram posts or rainbow-vomiting Snapchat videos will change that.

They don't determine your value. *You* determine your value. *You are always* worth everything.

DAY 14

August 31, 2017

Addy,

Set a good example. You're a role model to someone.

Love,
Dad

I learned this early on in my professional career when I was finishing graduate school and getting my first full-time job. Someone is always watching what you do. I don't want to be a role model to anyone because I'm not perfect, but I know my kids look up to me.

My kids mimic me. When I say or do something, Addison will sometimes retort with something I've told her before. *They do listen!*

As a big sister, Ashleigh and I constantly remind Addison that Jackson is always watching what she does—when he's not annoying the hell out of her. He loves his big sister and wants to do all the things she does, but he doesn't understand why he can't.

Whether you're an older sibling, a parent, a teammate, or the barista at my neighborhood coffeehouse, always set a good example. You may be the role model for someone you didn't realize.

WRITING EXERCISE

As adults, there are many things we wish we were told while we were growing up. Take ten minutes to list three lessons you wish you knew as a kid.

How can you adapt those lessons to help your child?

_____

_____

_____

_____

_____

_____

_____

_____

_____

_____

_____

_____

_____

DAY 15

September 1, 2017

Addy,

Your friends will try to pressure you into doing things. You don't have to do what everyone else is doing.

Love,
Dad

Friends are great to have. I've gained many, I've lost many. Despite the people I've encountered in my life, I've succumbed to their pressure several times. My skin is already itching at the thought that Addison's teenage years are around the corner.

I remember what it was like to be a teenager. Ashleigh remembers too. We know how intoxicating peer pressure can be or to be in a situation where you want to fit in. I want my daughter to be strong-willed and not easy to relent or give in.

Just because your friend is doing something doesn't mean you should as well. Sometimes a good friendship means being the yin to someone else's yang.

DAY 16

September 5, 2017

Addy,

Do what you love. Love what you do.

Love,
Dad

Slowly but surely, Addison started to find her stride in fourth grade. One day, she came home in a flurry of excitement.

"I joined 4-H! I also ran for secretary, and I won it, but I don't know what a secretary does. What does a secretary do?"

Ashleigh and I were elated to learn that our introverted nine-year-old was branching out and doing things that neither one of us would have done at her age.

Of course, our daughter later told us before one of her brother's soccer games, "So I decided I wanted to run for student council representative for my class."

"That's great, Add!" my wife chimed. "We can decorate posters, and your daddy can help you with a great campaign speech!"

I jokingly said she should run on the Free Candy Machine ticket.

"Well, we can't make posters, and we already had elections last week. I didn't win," Addison said matter-of-factly.

She shrugged her shoulders, asked for some money for the concession stand, and off she went.

I looked at my wife and asked, "What just happened?"

DAY 17

September 6, 2017

Addy,

Never be afraid to fail. That's the only way we learn.

Love,
Dad

There's no worse feeling of failure than being fired or losing a job. It took me almost a year to deduce what I learned from my biggest failure. That's why I decided to begin writing notes to Addison. I was not a strong father when we moved back to Louisiana after I lost my job.

I myself was lost. I was applying for job after job, getting rejection after rejection. I kept waking up every morning and trying again, not because I was a glutton for punishment but because I had to. I had to for my wife and kids. There were many mornings I didn't want to wake up or get out of bed because I felt like this nightmare was never going to end.

I was at rock bottom. After more than one hundred job applications and what I presume were more than one hundred rejections, I changed a few things and the nightmare ended. I wasn't afraid to fail. To me, I had already suffered the ultimate failure, so anything else was just extra practice.

In baseball, a .300 batting average is worthy of the Baseball Hall of Fame. In life, you only have to be right once to overcome the ninety-nine wrongs.

DAY 18

September 7, 2017

Addy,

What has four eyes but can't see? Mississippi.
Laugh! Have a great day!

Love,
Dad

    I thought this was pretty funny on a fourth-grade level. Ashleigh laughed. Jackson laughed only because his momma laughed. Addison?
    "Mississippi's a state. Of course, it can't see."
    Dammit, you are my kid.

DAY 19

September 8, 2017

Addy,

Worrying is like a rocking chair. It gives you something to do, but it doesn't get you anywhere (Van Wilder).

Love,
Dad

I almost stopped writing notes to Addison after this one when Ryan Reynolds, the actor who played Van Wilder, retweeted my #DadLunchNotes post on Twitter. *Swoon.*

I must be nineteen inside because I still laugh hysterically and uncontrollably when I watch *Van Wilder*. And his quote is one of the handful of quotes I memorized and regurgitate on a moment's notice because it's true.

As someone who has battled anxiety for a good portion of my adult life, I worry about things—many of which I cannot control. And I love a good rocking chair. Combine two of my favorite things, and I'm not going anywhere. Sitting in my rocking chair in my backyard is relaxing, for sure, but I stay in the same place.

I'm not moving forward or backward. I'm where I started. Worrying does the same thing. It gives you something to do, but it doesn't get you anywhere.

DAY 20

September 1, 2017

Addy,

To move forward, sometimes you first have to move backwards. It's *okay*. Have fun!

Love,
Dad

To end last week, I told Addison that worrying is like a rocking chair and that it doesn't get you anywhere. To begin this week, I told her sometimes you have to move backward to move forward.

Am I directionally challenged? No. I'm being honest and showing my daughter there's more to life than just black and white.

A fun part of life is trying, overcoming the setbacks, and enjoying the rewards of perseverance.

DAY 21

September 12, 2017

Addy,

Make today a glitter-filled bag of rainbows and unicorn farts.

Love,
Dad

I'm trying my hardest to make her laugh, and I accomplished it today! Addison loves unicorns, and fourth-grade humor always somehow revolves around farting, so every day should be a glitter-filled bag of unicorn farts!

DAY 22

September 13, 2017

Addy,

You're lucky enough to be different from everyone else. You're my unicorn. Don't ever change.

Love,
Dad

When I was thinking about what to title this book, I was flipping through the notes I had written to Addison, and then I remembered this one.

Lucky enough.

We're lucky enough to be different from everyone else. We're lucky enough to each have our own set of talents and unique qualities.

I'm lucky enough to have the wife and kids I have.

I hope one day my kids will think they were lucky enough to have the parents they had.

DAY 23

September 14, 2017

Addy,

Be a learner, not a finisher.
We are all lifelong learners. We will never know everything.

Love,
Dad

"I'll never have to know any of this when I'm older."

That's what Addison said after one of her first science tests.

"Uh, yeah, you will. You may not have to know it verbatim for whatever job you have when you're older, but you'll need to have some working knowledge."

"Wait ... what? What if I want to work at McDonald's when I'm in high school?"

"It doesn't matter, Addison. Everything you learn in school builds on the next thing, and they all lead to having a purpose in your life."

"*Ugh.*"

Yes, this was an actual conversation with an actual nine-year-old.

We now live in a world where knowledge and education are questioned on a daily basis. Challenge yourself to be a lifelong learner, not a lifelong finisher. There's always something new to learn and explore.

DAY 24

September 15, 2017

Addy,

Right is right even if no one does it. Wrong is wrong even if everyone does it.
Right isn't always going to be popular, but it's better than wrong.

Love,
Dad

Four rights make a square, and two wrongs don't make a right.

I'd rather my kids be squares because they do the right things rather than people who try to right the wrongs they make when no one was watching.

I don't have any evidence to prove this axiom, but I do believe that many of us only do the right things when eyes are on us. We don't do what's right all the time. That is human nature, but it doesn't make it right.

Whether eyes are watching you or not, do what is right. It's called karma.

DAY 25

September 18, 2017

Addy,

The loudest voice in the room is rarely the smartest person. Don't raise your voice, improve your argument.

Love,
Dad

When the kids are at each other's throats or they are yelling at us because they aren't happy with a decision we made, our rebuttal is simple: *Don't raise your voice, improve your argument.*

Why is it that when we are unhappy with something that happens, we try to resolve the matter by raising our voices rather than having a civil discussion? I mean, there are viral social media videos about customers berating Starbucks employees for getting their quad venti triple mocha-frappa-latte-tea half-caff decaf eight-pump vanilla whatever wrong.

Raising your voice doesn't better a situation. It only makes it worse, and it brings attention to something that inevitably won't make you look good. Just because I can be the loudest person in the room doesn't make me the smartest person.

It only makes the loud, annoying person in the room.

More conflicts and arguments can be solved with less screaming and less ALL CAPS PASSIVE-AGGRESSIVE TEXT MESSAGES.

Try it.

DAY 26

September 19, 2017

Addy,

Let your smile change the world, but don't let the world change your smile. Always smile!

Love,
Dad

Since the moment she gave me her first smile, I've always loved it. Now that her smile is accented by her freckles, I love it even more. I was self-conscious about my freckles and smile as a kid, so I didn't do it very often. Quite honestly, everything in this book is the antithesis of what I was as a kid. I want my daughter to be the opposite of what I experienced.

Too many of our children's smiles are being changed by the world around them.

Change the world with your smile. Don't ever let the world change your smile.

DAY 27

September 20, 2017

Addy,

Not everyone will like you. Don't take it personally like I do. It's a reflection of them, not you. You are amazing!

Love,
Dad

I don't claim to have a fan club, but I do know at one point I had a hate club. It was the product of a nasty, toxic work environment at a previous employer. I let the idea that a small group of grown men hated me consume my thoughts for almost two years.

Eventually, I learned to let go. I let that weight go, and I felt my body lighten. My mind was clear. It was then I realized I cannot take it personally if someone doesn't like me. If someone doesn't like me, then that's a "you problem," not a "me problem."

And it's true. Let them miss out and not get to know you. That's their issue. Plus, if everyone liked you, then the world would be boring.

Focus on the people that do like you. Make the ones that don't like you realize they are missing out on something amazing: you.

DAY 28

September 21, 2017

Addy,

Be a girl with a mind, a woman with attitude, and a lady with class.

Love,
Dad

Anyone can be anything. Thankfully, my daughter grew out of the pink gender phase before kindergarten. I want her to be fearless, smart, independent, open-minded, and an all-around kick-ass woman. For far too long, men have been intimidated by strong, independent women. That's absolutely ridiculous.

That's not what we teach either of our kids.

We fear what we do not understand, and many men in today's society don't understand—or like—that women can be powerful, smart, independent, and strong. Women are not arm candy.

I always hated the saying "Behind every man is a strong woman." No, my wife is beside me, not behind me. My daughter is not arm candy. She is smart, funny, strong-willed, and independent.

She's going to make for one helluva woman. But she will do it with manners and class.

DAY 29

September 22, 2017

Addy,

Be someone everyone should get to know, not someone who wants to be well-known.
Popularity doesn't mean anything.

Love,
Dad

Do you know people, or do you *know-know* people? Do you know the difference? For a period in my career, I was fixated on being well-known. I thought that was the key to promotions, six-figure salaries, and achieving my professional dreams. Having the desire to be well-known or reach celebrity status can push other important things in your life to the side. It obstructs your vision; it obstructs your true purpose.

I wasn't putting as much effort into getting to know people. When I was at a national conference to accept an award in 2014, Ashleigh and I were walking through the hotel to leave for dinner, and we were stopped by at least ten people wanting to talk to me.

"Oh my god, you're famous!" my wife quipped, laughing.

I chuckled at her joke, but I didn't like the feeling of being the center of attention. I hated it. I realized what I had inadvertently created with the wrong vision. Two days later, I was to accept a national award, but I was starting to feel sick and nauseated every time I stood up.

I was suffering the first of what I realized were anxiety attacks. I didn't want to be popular. I simply wanted to crawl into a corner where no one would see me.

DAY 30

September 25, 2017

Addy,

Open your mind before you open your mouth.

Love,
Dad

Arguably, I'm one of the more open-minded people in my extended family. I never truly conformed to a specific set of ideals.

"Are you a registered Republican or a Democrat?"

"Um, I'm a registered voter."

If you could see the looks I get when I say that. I look at everything at face value. I *try* to erase my biases and create my own conclusions before I say anything. That's easier said than done at times, but it's like I wrote Addison earlier: don't listen to respond; listen to understand.

Oftentimes, we open our mouths without fully understanding a situation or a story. That generally leads to rumor, conjecture or is a projection of our own thoughts. Be a freethinker. Open your mind to the possibility of new things or changing your mind.

People change their underwear every day (hopefully), so why can't you open your mind to the potential of changing your mind?

DAY 31

September 26, 2017

Addy,

Have a goal or a dream? Be like a postage stamp—
stick to it until you get there.
Always dream big.

Love,
Dad

"Why would I want to be a postage stamp? They get stuck in mailboxes."

You're missing the point, Addison.

When I was in graduate school, I wrote down a crude timeline of where I wanted to be in my career at twenty-five, thirty, thirty-five, forty, forty-five. I wrote it on the back of a bar napkin in my apartment, because why would you buy paper towels when you could grab a stab of napkins at the bar? Duh.

The goals I wrote for each age milestone were not necessarily unattainable, but damn, they were lofty. I became obsessive over these age goals. So obsessive, in fact, that I drove myself into therapy, made my depression worse, and had two nervous breakdowns—one at twenty-nine and another at thirty-three.

Always dream big, but not at the price of your family or your well-being. If I had it all over to do again, I would have wadded up that napkin and thrown it away. I put too much pressure on myself.

I don't want my kids to put that kind of pressure on themselves. It's not healthy. I merely want them to dream big and attach themselves to a dream they think they can achieve.

DAY 32

September 27, 2017

Addy,

Imperfection is beautiful!
If we were all perfect, then life would be boring.
Be imperfect.

Love,
Dad

"Daddy, how do they get women so pretty on the cover of magazines?"

"Photoshop, Addy."

"That's wrong."

If my nine-year-old can see the lies in the perfection being peddled to us, then you know something's up. I don't want my nine-year-old daughter thinking she has to look like all these glamorous women on the cover of magazines or modeling photos online.

There is no such thing as perfection unless it's created in Photoshop. And even then, if you zoom in close enough, you'll find imperfection.

Perfection is unattainable and makes people do ugly things. Imperfection is beautiful.

DAY 33

September 28, 2017

Addy,

Always work hard and do things *on time*.
There's no such thing as turning in late work or
getting extra credit in the real world.

Love,
Dad

My wife will tell you that when it comes to work or school projects, I do things "obnoxiously" on time. I always started working on papers or research projects as soon as they were assigned because I wanted to give myself as much time as possible to do the best I could.

Procrastination isn't really my style, although I do dabble in the art from time to time.

Addison, we thought, was doing all her assignments on time for class. There was one particular assignment she received a lower grade because it was turned in two days late.

"Why did you turn this in late?"

"I forgot to turn it in on time."

"You knew about it for two weeks!"

"Whoops."

Since this exchange, she turns in everything early because she now knows there's no such thing as turning in late work in the real world.

DAY 34

September 29, 2017

Addy,

Always be kind to everyone you meet. You don't know what battles they are facing.

Love,
Dad

As someone who has battled depression for almost twenty years, I've discovered that depression does not discriminate. You can be rich, beautiful, famous, poor, or infamous. It doesn't matter, but you know what does? How you treat other people.

How you treat people matters.

Don't berate the barista for making your drink wrong. You don't know what's going on in their life. They are a human being. No reason to be mean to someone who messed up your overly complicated coffee order.

I worked at a big-box retailer during the holiday season (it rhymes with Shmarget), and I was horrified by how some customers treat people who work in retail. It's as if they look down upon them. I'm simply trying to make a few dollars to keep a roof over my family and to keep what's left of my sanity. For every five friendly customers, I'd meet two or three people who either hated life or hated that I worked at Shmarget.

At first, I was upset at how they treated me, but then I felt sorry for them. Man, your life must be empty if you have to unload your anger on a Shmarget employee.

Cleanup on aisle A34.

WRITING EXERCISE

Have you ever heard of a parenting audit? Neither have I, because I think I just made it up. Think about the things you do on a daily, monthly, or yearly basis for your kids. Do you make their lunch? Do you leave little notes here and there! Do you coach their sports team?

Write down simple things you would like to start doing for your kids. There are no wrong answers.

_____

_____

_____

_____

_____

_____

_____

_____

_____

_____

_____

_____

DAY 35

October 2, 2017

Addy,

The world is changed by your example, not your opinion. Be a great example.

Love,
Dad

Last month, I told Addison to change the world with her smile. This month, I'm telling her the world is changed by her example. Am I confusing? Not intentionally. Life is complexly simple like a Rubik's Cube.

We can change the world both with our smile and our example. It's easy to disarm people with either one or both. People are more apt at following our example. Everyone has an opinion, and thanks to social media, *everyone* has an opinion.

Those opinions aren't changing the world, but they are changing the way we think. Instead of talking, exemplify. Be the change you want to see in the world by setting a good example.

Remember, it's easy to mute other people's opinions, but it's not easy to mute people's actions.

DAY 36

October 3, 2017

Addy,

The six most powerful words are:
Thank you.
You're welcome.
I'm sorry.
We should always show gratitude and humility.

Love,
Dad

We don't say thank you enough. It's 2018, and I still send handwritten thank-you notes on monogrammed stationery.

We also don't apologize enough. We save face by deflecting or blaming someone else.

Gratitude and humility aren't weaknesses. They are strengths. Two of the strongest virtues you can possess.

I say thank you often, but I know I could be better. I don't apologize nearly as often as I should. I hardly admit I am wrong. The words "I'm sorry" don't roll off my tongue as easily as they should.

Be gracious in victory; be humble in defeat.

DAY 37

October 4, 2017

Addy,

You are beautiful.
You are kind.
You are loved.
You are enough.
You can do anything.

Love,
Dad

Sometimes it's nice to be reminded there are people who support us no matter what. This morning, I felt Addison needed a confidence boost. She is beautiful. No matter how often she yells at her brother, she is still kind.

Her family loves and adores her. She is enough. She can do anything.

I know there will be people who tell her she can't do something, but I want her to know that I believe she can do anything. Every day, I try to instill that idea in her.

You are enough.

DAY 38

October 5, 2017

Addy,

No matter how successful you become, people
will talk about you behind your back.
That's life. Remember this: they're behind you
for a reason.

Love,
Dad

Kids will be kids. They will tease others. They will talk about others behind their back. Adults will do the same too. There will always people who'd rather live in gossip and rumor rather than truth.

A few girls have been saying things about Addison behind her back. She can be quite shy and reserved, so at times, she won't stand up for herself. No matter how hard you try, people will always talk about you behind your back. That means you must be interesting, right?

Let them talk about you all they want. That means you have something they don't. When you're feeling low because it's happening to you, remember this: those that are talking behind your back, they're behind you for a reason.

DAY 39

October 6, 2017

Addy,

Anyone can be your hero.
If you look up to me, know than I am far from
perfect and I don't always make the best decisions.
I'm human.

Love,
Dad

Disclaimer: I don't want to be my kids' hero. Of course, I've never subscribed to the idea of "hero worship," but I know kids will always have adults they look up to or try to emulate. When kids choose a hero, they typically only see one side of that person—what that person *wants them to see*.

Take any professional athlete or actor for instance. What you see on the big screen or in an arena isn't necessarily who that person really is. Before you decide to choose someone as your hero or role model, see them for who they really are.

I'd rather my kids and others get the entire picture of who I really am rather than the facade of who they *think* I am.

DAY 40

October 9, 2017

Addy,

Knowledge is knowing what to say.
Wisdom is knowing whether or not to say it. We need both.

Love,
Dad

I know a lot about a lot of things. Some of it is completely useless information that is only good for trivia and dominating *Jeopardy!* However, I don't always have the wisdom of not saying something. There have been times when—as an adult—my mouth has gotten me in trouble. I'm not afraid to back down from an argument or insert myself somewhere where I don't necessarily belong. Some people may even say I have a smart mouth.

There are times when things are better left unsaid. Words have power, and that power can be debilitating to the person on the receiving end. There will be times when our words are necessary, and if we don't say them, then we are simply turning our back on the problem.

Yes, what we say may get us in trouble. But would you rather get in trouble for saying something you shouldn't or get in trouble for not saying something you should?

DAY 41

October 10, 2017

Addy,

There's enough negativity in the world.
If you don't have anything nice to say, then don't say it!

Love,
Dad

There are many aspects to wisdom. Wisdom, of course, is the ability to spread positive thoughts into the world. There's enough negative energy around us.

DAY 42

October 11, 2017

Addy,

Never be too old to learn and never be too young
to make a difference.

Love,
Dad

No matter the number of degrees or the number of awards you've received, you are never too old or too experienced to learn. Every day is a learning experience. But don't let your age or inexperience be the reason others use to say that you can't make a difference in someone's life.

She doesn't know, nor does she realize it, but Addison makes a difference in my life every day.

DAY 43

October 12, 2017

Addy,

You cannot make everyone happy. *You are not a taco*. But if you were a taco, then everyone would be happy … *and hungry!*

Love,
Dad

Taco … Thursday? I came up with this one a few days too late. It would have been a great Taco Tuesday note, but I had to settle for Thursday instead.

We cannot make everyone happy. It's humanly impossible. On the flip side, tacos make everyone happy. Can you imagine how happy we'd all be if we were tacos? Suddenly, I'm hungry.

DAY 44

October 13, 2017

Addy,

I'm so proud of you for how much you've grown as a volleyball player. As long as you have fun and are a great teammate, that's *all that matters!*

Love,
Dad

Addison stepped outside of her comfort zone and asked to play volleyball. In case you were wondering, she possesses my lack of athletic skill. For someone who had never touched a volleyball until ten minutes before her tryout, she improved a great deal.

Game after game, practice after practice, she kept trying. She never gave up. She kept putting forth the effort. That's what matters to me.

DAY 45

October 16, 2017

Addy,

Treat everyone like they're the most important person you'll ever meet.

Love,
Dad

They say you should never meet your heroes. They will be the ones to disappoint you the most.

We, too, often put people on pedestals. Sports fans wear the jerseys of their favorite players on their favorite teams. We are starstruck when we see a celebrity in person.

Celebrities are no different from you or me. The only difference is that they make more money than we do. Stop worshipping celebrities.

Start treating regular people like superstars. They are the most important people you'll ever meet.

DAY 46

October 17, 2017

Addy,

Every day, we have two choices:
Get better or get worse. Never stay the same.
Choose to *win the day*.

Love,
Dad

I borrowed this from one of our local high school principals. I had heard variations of similar axioms during my career. A similar thought that my dad always shared with me on a semiregular basis while I was in college and early on in my career: "Every day is a job interview."

He is certainly correct. Since my daughter is only nine and it is against the law for her to have a job, I went with this one from the principal. We're given a choice every day. The choice is on us. We can get better or worse. We will never remain the same. We may feel stagnant in our job or in our life, but in reality, we can only do two things—get better or get worse.

To me, if you "stay the same," then you aren't getting better. Think of it like the fuel gauge in your car—you deplete your tank, but then you fill it up. You either get better (full tank) or worse (empty tank).

The choice is yours.

DAY 47

October 18, 2017

Addy,

Words have *power*. When you say something, *mean it*.

Love,
Dad

Looking back on everything I've written Addison this year, I unconsciously was writing in a particular pattern. Many of my notes centered on words. I wrote words on a sticky note about the power of words and how words can either help or hurt people.

People have hurt me with their words, but their words have also helped me. I have hurt people with my words, but I've also been able to uplift others—I hope. Words are not empty thoughts. There's always something tucked away in everything we say.

Before you unload a long-winded epithet about someone, take a ten-second cooling-off period. Is this worth it? Do I really mean what I'm about to say? How would I feel if someone said it to me?

I think we forget that everyone has feelings—even those who appear to not.

DAY 48

October 19, 2017

Addy,

Finishing first doesn't count unless you're in the Olympics.
Don't rush.
Take your time.
Do your best.
School isn't a competition. You're more than a letter grade.

Love,
Dad

I don't care about grades (although I'm obsessively ridiculous about my grades in college). I've told my kids I don't care about grades. I care about *effort*. Did you try your very best? If your very best is a C, then good job! If you only gave 60 percent effort and you got a C, then we have problems.

Focus on doing the best you can. Not everyone can be valedictorian in their graduating class. Not everyone is going to get a full scholarship to a prestigious Ivy League institution. The only thing we can control is *our effort*. All I ever ask of my kids is to give their all in everything they do.

I don't care about grades, awards, or scholarships. I care about your best.

DAY 49

October 20, 2017

Addy,

Focus first on being interested in others before being interesting to others.

Love,
Dad

We live in a *me, me, me* world. As typical twenty-first-century parents, we gave our kids an opportunity to have their own tablets for their use. They were given specific parameters and rules to follow. The moment they went out of bounds, they lost their privileges. After several months, we began noticing a trend in their sleep patterns, moods, and eating habits.

Ashleigh and I took them away, and they haven't had them in almost a year. They were no longer interested in the outside world. They were only interested in burying their heads in videos and games.

Like me, I think Addison used technology as her safety blanket. I'm not going to lie or pontificate—I, too, hide behind my phone when I feel uncomfortable or don't want to socialize. However, how are you going to ever meet people if you don't unleash yourself into the wild of society?

Put your phone down. Make an effort and be interested in others. Once they see how interested you are in them, they might think you're pretty interesting yourself.

DAY 50

October 23, 2017

Addy,

Scars are like tattoos but with better stories.

Love,
Dad

No, my daughter does not have a tattoo, but I do. I have a semicolon on the inside of my life wrist to remind me to *breathe*. A few times in my life, I have contemplated suicide because I thought life was too hard for me to navigate and that my family would be better off without me. I'll admit—that story is deep. Most times when people ask me about it, I tell them I am a grammar nerd (which I am), and the semicolon is my favorite punctuation. (*Don't tell that to the interrobang, though. He'll get jealous!*)

Last night, as Addison was clearing out the dishwasher, I heard a loud crash, followed by a bloodcurdling scream. I raced into the kitchen to find my daughter's foot resting in a puddle of blood. We rushed to the nearest emergency room, and she was petrified of what was next. I lay next to her in the hospital bed as the doctors placed two stitches in her foot to close up the deep gash opened by a thick shard of glass.

See, her story is better than mine.

DAY 51

October 24, 2017

Addy,

Always do the right thing even when no one is looking. It's called integrity.

Love,
Dad

Don't be the person who only does good things or the right thing when people are watching or if the cameras are rolling. That's not being a good citizen. That's called being a good faker.

Don't do it.

DAY 52

October 25, 2017

Addy,

Life isn't fair.
Many times, you will feel like you were cheated.
Instead of complaining about what you *don't have*, be grateful for what you *do have*.

Love,
Dad

"It's not fair."

I know every parent has heard that refrain from their children at some point. We've heard it a few too many times. Addison's comment came the day after someone in her class got picked to do something.

"Addison, life isn't fair. Not everyone will get picked to do something, and not everyone will get a participation trophy."

Addison paused and looked at me. I continued.

"Does so-and-so have this, this, or this?" I said as I point to some things around the house.

"I-I don't think so," Addison said. "I get what you're saying."

Life isn't fair. It never has been fair, and it never will be. Rather than bemoan what's going wrong for you, celebrate what's going right.

DAY 53

October 26, 2017

Addy,

You can do *anything*, but you cannot do *everything*. You are enough.

Love,
Dad

Too many people try to be too many things to too many people. I struggle trying to be a husband, dad, employee, college student, and part-time sports coach. It's exhausting.

I want my kids to strive for greatness. I want them to be whatever they want to be, but to be everything is impossible. During the school semester, I'm exhausted—mentally, physically, and emotionally. I don't want my kids to ever have to juggle so many things at once.

You can do anything you want, but be reasonable. You are enough.

DAY 54

October 27, 2017

Addy,

When you're wrong, *admit it*.
When you're right, *be quiet*.

Love,
Dad

I have many bad habits, but when it comes to my family, my worst habit is my relentless desire to get the last word in every conversation. Not only do I always aim to get the last word in every conversation; I sometimes have a problem admitting when I'm wrong.

I know, I know. I'm not winning any "Dad of the Year" trophies with these confessions, but I'm admitting it now. When I'm wrong, I don't necessarily admit it—right away, at least. When I'm right, I don't always stay quiet—not so humblebrag.

Be humble in victory and gracious in defeat.

DAY 55

October 30, 2017

Addy,

It doesn't matter how many times you fail.
You only have to be right *once*.

Love,
Dad

I love baseball. Despite Addison's dislike of sports—she'll still watch games with me and ask questions—I'll use baseball metaphors around the house. Baseball is a great example of how we only have to be right once to be successful.

Never stop trying. Never give up on your dream.

If you strike out in your first ninety-nine at bats and you get the game-winning hit in your one hundredth at bat, people will talk about how you overcame adversity in the biggest moment—not how you failed the first ninety-nine times.

Keep walking up to the plate.

You only have to get a hit once.

DAY 56

October 31, 2017

Addy,

Be a voice, not an echo. (Speak up for others, don't simply speak after.)

Love,
Dad

Like.
Retweet.
Comment.
Share.
That's communication in 2018. It's both a good thing and a disastrous one too. With the immediacy of communication, factions of people have gained a voice, while other factions have lost theirs. Some people are simply echoes in a vast echo chamber known as the internet.

Don't pile onto someone else's thoughts. Be your own voice. Draw your own conclusions.

Speak up for others; don't simply speak after others.

Be a voice, not an echo.

WRITING EXERCISE

Turn on social media. I'm sure you'll find some funny posts, some heartwarming photos, gut-wrenching posts, and some things that'll make you seethe with anger.

I started posting #DadLunchNotes on Twitter, Facebook, and Instagram to try to shed some positive light into an otherwise negative world. How can you use your social media voice for social good?

_____

_____

_____

_____

_____

_____

_____

_____

_____

_____

_____

_____

DAY 57

November 1, 2017

Addy,

Anything is possible. Either find a way or make one.

Love,
Dad

Rarely am I at a loss for words. This was one of those occasions where I had no rhyme or reason for what I wrote. I just wrote how I felt that morning.

DAY 58

November 2, 2017

Addy,

The difference between *ordinary* and *extraordinary* is a little *extra*. You, my girl, are *extraordinary*!

Love,
Dad

I've been a college adjunct instructor on the side for the last few years. One semester—my first semester teaching, in fact—I had a student who didn't turn in the first two assignments. However, she managed to do well on the midterm and the final exams while also turning in her other assignments on time. Based on her point average, she earned a midrange B for the course.

Less than an hour after submitting the final grades,

she sent me an e-mail.

"Mr. Yandle, I noticed you gave me a B for the class, but I feel as though I deserve an A. Is there any way I could do extra credit to boost my grade?"

My first thought, *That's ballsy.*

My second—and real—response was this: You failed to turn in not one but two assignments at the beginning of the semester. Because of that, you get a B.

Why can't people take accountability for their inability to do things they are expected or required to do? No one wants to go the extra mile and give more than what's asked of them. Yet when the deadline passes or the grades are turned, they ask for extra time or for extra credit.

DAY 59

November 3, 2017

Addy,

You are the exclamation mark in the happiest sentence I could ever write!

Love,
Dad

I wanted to put a smile on my daughter's face. She truly is the exclamation mark at the end of the happiest sentence I've ever written. This book you're reading now is for her. It's because of her.

I don't use exclamation points often because I don't like people shouting at me while I'm reading! But every time I use one, I think of her!

DAY 60

November 6, 2017

Addy,

The more you step up, you step out of the crowd.
You're too *bright* not to stand out!

Love,
Dad

When I was younger, I was too timid to step out from the crowd. I didn't like the attention—I still don't. As I progressed through middle school and then through high school, I remained—for the most part—in the background. I was involved in a few organizations, not many. I surely wasn't running for any positions. I think that purposeful approach to staying in the crowd aided to my fear of public speaking and being in front of large groups.

Once I started college, I slowly started to realize that blending in with the crowd didn't "protect" me from anything. It only hurt me from experiencing opportunities and be exposed to skills I needed.

At first, it'll be tough to overcome your anxiety and the fear of being in front of your peers. After a while, it'll feel natural.

Your star is too bright not to be on display for everyone else to see.

DAY 61

November 7, 2017

Addy,

Perfect people aren't real, and real people aren't perfect.

Love,
Dad

For the first part of my career, I was chasing job titles and perfection. At the same time, I was trying to be the perfect husband and the perfect father. You'll be surprised to learn that I was indeed not perfect at any of these. It was the first of my five therapists—yes, five—that I learned about the false sense of perfection.

Perfection does not exist. Those who chase perfection will only feed their insatiable appetite for needing to be perfect. It's unattainable. If we chase perfection, then we engage in an endless cycle of ups and downs.

People who portray themselves as having the perfect life are trying to mask the pain of what's missing. Don't do that because you're setting yourself up for a life filled with misery.

DAY 62

November 8, 2017

Addy,

Don't listen to simply respond with your opinion.
Listen to understand.

Love,
Dad

Here I go with listening more and talking less again. As parents, we engage in constant debates with our children over right and wrong. Inevitably, they end up talking back when we're talking to them and vice versa. Most of the time—without realizing it—we're all not listening to the entire conversation.

We're listening to small pieces of the conversation, pieces that we care about. We tune out the minutiae of the moment. That often leads to miscommunication and misunderstanding. Yet my six-year-old son who is obsessed with watching sports on TV and watches day-old game replays at 6:00 a.m. on Saturdays asked me one morning,

"Daddy, why are those guys screaming at each other on TV?"

I look up, and it's the barking carnival, otherwise known as one of the handfuls of morning sports talk shows.

My six-year-old may not listen to everything we say before he responds, but he's old enough to know that we get nothing from carnival barkers.

DAY 63

November 9, 2017

Addy,

Be somebody who makes everybody feel like
somebody.

Love,
Dad

I think it's more important to make someone else feel important
rather than someone making you feel important. In order to lift
ourselves up, we should lift others up first. It's like the popular
aphorism: "A rising tide lifts all boats."

Be the tide that lifts the other boats washed ashore in the harbor.
If you think about it, each one of us is a boat that either is lost at sea
or has been washed ashore and unable to get back in the water.

Be that tide. Be that person that does the lifting up. Don't beat
others down for your personal gain. Lifting others up will get you
much further in life.

DAY 64

November 10, 2017

Addy,

Expect *nothing*.
Appreciate *everything*.

Love,
Dad

I have a stack of personalized note cards that sit on my desk at the house. This is probably my sixth or seventh iteration of these cards. During the course of any given year, I'll handwrite as many as one hundred different cards to people I know in various places as an act of gratitude and appreciation for other people.

It could be for their friendship, their guidance, their mentorship, or my favorite—just because.

This act of gratitude helps center me and collect my thoughts when I've had trouble finding my way.

And when birthdays and Christmastime come around, both of our kids are required to write handwritten thank-you notes to those who gave those gifts.

Expect *nothing*. Appreciate *everything*.

DAY 65

November 13, 2017

Addy,

Life is full of enough problems. Your life should be full of solutions.

Love,
Dad

When I was a boss, I told my staff, "If you come into my office with a problem, then you better come with a solution too."

It's easy for all of us to point out the problems in life or the problems in our workplace. But do you know what's hard to do? Coming up with solutions to those problems.

If coming up with solutions were easy, then we'd all have our problems solved before we complained about those problems. I want my kids to be problem-solvers and critical thinkers, not complainers filled with malaise.

Anytime Addison comes to us with a problem or a complaint, we ask her, "What can you do to fix it?"

We want her to think about a situation. We want to give our kids the tools they need to succeed in life. You can't Google everything. I mean, you could Google this if you wanted to, but I'm sure there will be some cat videos that pop up too.

DAY 66

November 14, 2017

Addy,

You are the company you keep. Be careful who surrounds you.

Love,
Dad

It was around this time when we realized that some of the problems Addison was experiencing at schools were directly and indirectly related to some of the people she associated herself with. As I got older, I learned that people will make snap judgments not only on your work and your looks but also based on the people you associate with. You know how many people I purged from my Facebook friends list after I learned that tidbit?

Who you befriend and associate with does affect you. It may not affect you directly, but it may affect you indirectly. Nowadays, it's not necessarily who you know but who those people know. If you can play the game Six Degrees of Separation and connect yourself with someone that you're unsure of, then you know you need to make some changes.

I'm not telling you to ghost or unfriend everyone in your life. I'm saying to be careful with who surrounds you. You become the company you keep.

DAY 67

November 15, 2017

Addy,

When someone does something wrong, don't forget all the things they did right.

Love,
Dad

There are obviously some exceptions to this suggestion, but for the most part, it's an important thing to remember.

I've done plenty of wrong things, but—thankfully—Ashleigh remembers the things I did right. While both of my kids have the memory of an elephant, they remember my wrongs and my rights. And my speeding tickets.

Be sure to forgive others, but don't forget what they did or how they made you feel.

DAY 68

November 16, 2017

Addy,

You miss 100 percent of the shots you don't take.
Wayne Gretzky
Michael Scott
Daddy

Love,
Dad

I tried my hardest to insert some humor from one of my favorite TV shows, *The Office*.

"Daddy, are you feeling okay? I don't get this. Who's Wayne Gretzky?"

It was an epic face-palm emoji moment.

"I told you she wouldn't get it," Ashleigh said.

I should listen to my wife more often.

DAY 69

November 17, 2017

Addy,

Not everyone is destined for greatness, but we can all try to be great.

Love,
Dad

Everyone's definition of *great* is different. We can all dare to be great because your great is not the same as my great. We all bring differing levels of greatness, but we cannot all be at the top of the greatness mountain.

Aim to be your level of great.

DAY 70

November 27, 2017

Addy,

You are like a diamond.
Bright.
Strong.
Resilient.
Beautiful.

Love,
Dad

My three favorite diamonds are my wife's engagement ring, her earrings, and my daughter. All three of them are bright, strong, resilient, and beautiful. Of course, I think Addison is the most beautiful of the three.

Yes, a girl's best friend is a diamond. The next best thing to giving your wife or daughter a diamond? Telling her she's as beautiful as one.

DAY 71

November 28, 2017

Addy,

You will never influence the world by trying to be like everyone else.

Love,
Dad

If we were all the same, the world would be a boring place. If we were all the same, how would we be able to influence one another? We couldn't. We'd all be minions. We are able to influence others by not being like other people.

We cannot learn from people who are just like us. We may experience some short-term gains in the beginning, but eventually, we'll plateau and we won't get any better. Find someone who thinks differently than you. Find someone who challenges what you do, challenges what you think, and challenges what you believe. You can both influence each other.

Attention and time are the most precious commodity in our world. It's more precious than any gemstone or precious metal. Treat your influence—or your potential influence ability—the same way.

DAY 72

November 29, 2017

Addy,

Life is tough, but you know what? So are you, baby girl!

Love,
Dad

With the second quarter winding down, we were hitting some roadblocks both in school and at home. Addison's confidence was bumpy and bouncing all over the place. She was questioning her abilities in school, and her grades were reflecting that. We knew she wasn't giving us her best.

It was important that I reiterate to her that she's a tough cookie. She's like a coconut—hard on the outside and sweet on the inside. Once she cracks, you don't want to let her go. However, I want her to grow up to be a strong, independent woman.

We can't be there every moment of the school day. We have to let them go each morning. They are stronger than we think.

DAY 73

November 30, 2017

Addy,

A face without *freckles* is like a night without *stars*. I love your freckles!

Love,
Dad

When I was eight or nine, my parents took us to the water park on a summer vacation.

While we were slathering on sunscreen to attack the summer Alabama heat, an older woman walked up to me and said, "You look like you swallowed a dollar and broke out in pennies!"

It took me a few years to realize what she meant. As a kid, my face was covered in freckles. *Duh!* Addison's face hasn't broken a dollar bill—yet—but freckles do paint her face from cheek to cheek. Ashleigh has freckles too. Over time, I learned to embrace my freckles, although I was teased as a kid for having them. *It's not my fault!*

Even when the sky is cloudy, you can still make out the stars in the night. I couldn't imagine a face without freckles.

WRITING EXERCISE

This time of a year is a time for thanks. Gratitude gives us the right attitude. Take a few minutes to write down what you're thankful for in your life. I won't look.

DAY 74

December 1, 2017

Addy,

I may not say it enough, but my greatest accomplishment in life is being your dad.

Love,
Dad

I don't care about fame, awards, or accolades. At various times in my younger career, I was constantly chasing awards, promotions, and pay raises because I *thought* those were the epitome of success and accomplishment. All this time, my accomplishments were always in front of me—you, your brother, your mother, and the way we raise you in an effort to become extraordinary people.

You are a beautiful and smart little girl who is quickly growing up into a young woman. I am struggling with the thought of losing my baby girl, but no matter how many times you and I argue, butt heads, and disagree, nothing will ever take away from how proud I am of you.

DAY 75

December 4, 2017

Addy,

Kindness is a language which deaf people can hear and the blind can see.

Love,
Dad

I don't know sign language. I cannot read sign language. I cannot read Braille either. I do—however—know how to read and speak the language of kindness. Truth be told, I don't always practice what I preach, and I am not always the kindest person in the room.

No matter the circumstance, kindness is the right thing. It's the only thing that all of us understand.

DAY 76

December 5, 2017

Addy,

Don't worry about fitting into glass slippers.
I want you to focus on breaking glass ceilings!
#girlpower

> Love,
> Dad

You can't do this because you're a girl. You can't do that because you're a girl. Want to dream? Dream you are a princess with a sparkling tiara and brittle glass slippers.

Give. Me. A. Break.

Princesses are cute when they are four or five, but my daughter isn't going to grow up to become a princess. I don't want her believing in or conforming to the gender norms that we've pushed upon our kids for decades. I-I can't do it. I want my daughter being one of the women shattering glass ceilings and opening doors for women to be successful.

Girl power.

DAY 77

December 6, 2017

Addy,

Our actions affect everyone around us.
Before we say or do, we must *think*.

Love,
Dad

Sir Isaac Newton said that "every action results in an equal or opposite reaction." While I'm not giving my daughter physics lessons in fourth grade, I want her to know that everything she does will affect more than just her. Your actions today may not affect the people around us today, but they will have an effect on them eventually.

Before we say or do anything, we must first think about our actions. Sometimes life moves too fast for us to think before we act. Sometimes we think after we act. It happens.

DAY 78

December 11, 2017

Addy,

Never lie to someone who trusts you, and never trust someone who lies to you.
Lying is never worth it.

Love,
Dad

Kids lie. I think it's a requirement. I lied when I was a kid—especially if it meant saving my butt from trouble. Our kids lie to us, but they always get caught.

As I tried to explain to Addison one day, "How would you feel if your best friend lied to you?"

"I wouldn't like it."

"Okay, how do you think I feel when you lie to me?"

"You don't like it?"

"No, I don't."

If someone you love or care about is on the other end of the lie you are about to tell, are they worth it? Is the lie you are about to tell worth saving your butt for a few extra seconds?

Lies always come around in the end. Always.

DAY 79

December 12, 2017

Addy,

You can't improve if you constantly aim for perfection.
Perfection is impossible.
Aim for awesome and you'll always improve.

Love,
Dad

As a full-blooded perfectionist, it is often hard to me to accept a project as is, knowing that's as good as it's going to get. I've already rewritten this page five—now, six—times. Perfection is impossible.

Ashleigh and I had the *perfect* wedding. It wasn't because everything in the church was situated perfectly or the food at the reception was *c'est magnifique*. The deacon called my wife Jennifer—remember, her name is Ashleigh—three times, so our wedding was not perfect by the very definition.

It was perfect because she was there next to me. It was perfect because it was the beginning of our life together. That day was awesome.

Being awesome is perfection. Being perfect is awesomely impossible.

DAY 80

December 13, 2017

Addy,

In our world, good doesn't always defeat evil. But
most days, good prevails.
Always do good!

Love,
Dad

When Addison read this, she wanted to point out my incorrect grammar.

"Daddy! Your grammar is wrong—it's 'Always do *well*', not *good*."

I told her she wasn't wrong, and I wasn't either.

"Doing good means doing good deeds for others. Doing good means you're helping others. Do *well* in school, but do *good* for others."

She shrugged her shoulders.

"I'm still going to say you're wrong because you aren't wrong often."

Addison – 1, Daddy – 0.

DAY 81

December 14, 2017

Addy,

What you say is not nearly as important as what you hear.

Love,
Dad

Here I go with another "listen more, talk less" message. What I write in this book is not nearly as important as what I hear from my wife or kids—unless it's about me being wrong.

When you sit down for dinner tonight, ask your kids a simple question: What did you do today? And let them take the wheel from there. Listen to them. Listen to every word, every *um* and *uh*. Actively listen to them. If they know you're not listening to them, then they won't want to share with you.

DAY 82

December 15, 2017

Addy,

Always remember:
You are braver than you believe,
Stronger than you seem, and
Smarter than you think.

Love,
Dad

This is one of my favorite quotes from A. A. Milne.

DAY 83

December 18, 2017

Addy,

You're never too important to be nice to people.
Always be nice, giving, and loving.

Love,
Dad

How many times have you said "I'm too busy" for someone? Is your hand up? You can't see mine, but both of my hands are in the air. I'm equally as guilty for being "too busy" to make time for someone else.

We all have crazy, jam-packed, overscheduled lives among the kids, work, bills, after-school activities, sports, marriage, and life in general. No wonder we're all exhausted and drink eight cups of coffee every morning.

I've missed out on some friendships and relationships in my life because I was focused on other areas. I didn't make time for people who supported me. My circle of friends has shrunk drastically over the past few years, mostly on purpose but partly because I ignored them. Additionally, with the "extra room" in my life, I still wasn't making time for others.

I wasn't too important for people—I was just acting that way.
Never be too important for other people.

DAY 84

December 19, 2017

Addy,

A smile is the best makeup a girl can wear.

Love,
Dad

We're halfway through fourth grade, and all I can think about is, she's less than three years away from junior high school. Before I know it, she's going to be all grown-up and will want nothing to do with me!

Dads, we are the most important male figures in our daughters' lives. Always provide that positive affirmation. Remind them what beauty really is and how real men should treat women.

Makeup isn't necessary.

WRITING EXERCISE

As the calendar turns to another year, everyone's minds flock to resolutions. I don't like resolutions. I start each new year with goals: What do I want to do this year? How do I want to get better this year? What goals do you want to start this year?

_____

_____

_____

_____

_____

_____

_____

_____

_____

_____

_____

_____

DAY 85

January 3, 2018

Addy,

Be sure to taste your words before you spit them out. Words have power.

Love,
Dad

The holiday break was tough in our household. Ashleigh and I finally unearthed some of things Addison had been dealing with at school and what had caused her sudden change in demeanor over the past few months. It came to a head the night before the kids were set to go back to school. It was far from my finest moment as a father.

There was screaming. There was crying.

For an hour, I sat quietly on the couch while I held Addison, who was crying intermittently. Finally, she cracked. She didn't tell me everything that was going on, but she gave me enough to work with.

Now, we were entering an area in which Ashleigh and I experienced far too often as kids—bullying.

During the tantrum-filled night, Addison said things she didn't mean. We know she didn't mean them, but what she said led to what I wrote her the next morning.

Don't say something to someone without knowing how it's going to make that person feel. Words have power—an immense power. You cannot see words, but sometimes they taste awful when they come out of your mouth.

DAY 86

January 4, 2018

Addy,

Eyes are useless when the mind is blind. Keep both open.

Love,
Dad

None of us are completely open-minded. Many of us walk like we're blind because our heads are buried in our mobile devices. When it comes to critical thinking, it's important to keep your eyes and your mind open. If we can't do this as parents, then how can we expect our children to do the same?

Our kids mimic our decisions and our beliefs. We are the ultimate influencers in their lives. Help them open their eyes and minds by opening your own.

DAY 87

January 5, 2018

Addy,

Whatever you are, I am too. (That's a good thing.)

Love,
Dad

My daughter is my twin. There's a semistrong resemblance in the face (according to my wife), and we have many of the same mannerisms. When I was her age, I was petrified at the possibility of turning out like my parents or my grandparents. I grew up being constantly compared to my older sister and others, so I think I was trying to create a proactive campaign against it.

As I've grown older, I've—slowly—accepted the notion that it's a good thing if your kids turn out like you. I want both of my kids to be better versions of my wife and me. This was a subtle reminder that no matter what she is or who she becomes, I am the same thing.

DAY 88

January 8, 2018

Addy,

I've failed more times than you'll ever know.
I've lost friends and ruined relationships because
of my decisions.
No matter how many times I fail, I'm always
scared to try again.
It's *okay* to be scared. It's *okay* to be afraid.
But it's not *okay* not to try!

Love,
Dad

If I knew then what I know now, there are certainly things I wouldn't do again and decisions I would change. When I had the chance to become a boss at the ripe age of thirty, I was told I was ready. I thought I was ready. It couldn't be too hard, right?

Boy was I wrong. My first two years as a boss weren't easy, but I was able to carefully navigate pitfalls and mitigate issues for the betterment of my staff. When I left for another job to take over another office, I didn't know I was walking into a fiery pit of failure.

This time, I wasn't afraid to take on being a boss at a new place. However, this is one of the decisions I wish I had done differently. After failing miserably at this second act of leadership, I became jaded. I was reluctant to try new things, but I kept moving.

No matter how many times failure hits us, we have to hit back.

DAY 89

January 9, 2018

Addy,

Be a fountain, not a drain.

Love,
Dad

"Why would I want to be a drain?"

"No, I want you to be a *fountain*, not a drain."

A fountain is a wellspring of water. People flock to fountains. Fountains are full of energy. They are contagious. Drains are energy suckers. They drain us of happiness and positive energy.

Which one do you think people want to surround themselves with?

Fountains. Drains are dangerous.

Be a fountain, not a drain.

DAY 90

January 10, 2018

Addy,

When you become lazy, it's disrespectful to those who believe in you. Don't be lazy.

Love,
Dad

We're still trying to pinpoint the exact problems that have resulted in Addison's abrupt change in demeanor. I shouldn't call my kids lazy, but this morning, I did. Being lazy is disrespectful to others.

It's okay to have an "off day" or take a slower approach because you're tired, but never be lazy.

DAY 91

January 11, 2018

Addy,

Treat people the way you want to be treated.
Respect is *earned*, not given.

Love,
Dad

There are people in your life that may treat you like an ATM machine—they take, take, and take. That's all they do. They don't give. They don't deposit anything into other people's accounts.

You can't expect respect from other people if you view it as a one-sided relationship. You're not making an ATM withdrawal. Every interaction with another person is an investment—an investment of time and emotion.

Sometimes we make bad investments. Sometimes our investments don't mature. Sometimes we overdraw our accounts. In order to make money, you must spend money. In order to avoid overdraft fees, you need to deposit more money.

Money doesn't equal respect, but respect is money (earned).

DAY 92

January 12, 2018

Addy,

You don't have to accept the things that you're not *okay* with or are wrong.
Stand up for yourself!

Love,
Dad

At the end of the day, the only person that can look after you is you. We don't have to accept things at face value. It's *okay* to not be *okay* with something.

If you're being mistreated or something doesn't feel right, *stand up*. At the end of the day, you are the only one who can stand up for yourself.

DAY 93

January 24, 2018

Addy,

Be yourself because an original is worth more than
a copy. Have a great day!

Love,
Dad

Authenticity wins every single time. You can copy others, but
you're robbing people at the chance of seeing an original. Anyone can
be a copy. Anyone can be a generic of the real thing.

Be yourself. Be an original version. Don't be anybody else.

Be you.

DAY 94

January 25, 2018

Addy,

You belong to a long line of women who began
as girls dreaming.
And they grew up to make a difference. *Dream*.

Love,
Dad

At this point in the school year, I was becoming creatively exhausted. There were several nights I'd fall asleep with a great idea in my mind, but I'd wake up with a blank mind. I'd stare at my notepad like my starving kids stare at me when they're hungry in the morning.

Not only was I putting pressure on myself to perform with a pen, but I was beginning to lose sight of why I did this every morning—for Addison.

This struggle would come and go during the final four months of the school year. You'll notice some of my writer's block days in the coming pages.

DAY 95

January 30, 2018

Addy,

Always ask questions.
The greatest learning is in what we don't see at
first.

Love,
Dad

My kids think I'm a walking encyclopedia. When Addison was little, I earned the nickname "Yandlepedia" from some coworkers at my office because it seemed like I knew the answer to everything. I've always had the desire to learn new things and have a vast wealth of knowledge.

Here's a bit of irony: I don't like asking questions. I feel like I'm imposing on others with superfluous questions. While I dislike asking questions, Ashleigh and I highly encourage our kids to ask questions.

We don't have all the answers at first. The real answers may be found with further questioning and not easily seen with our eyes at first. *Always ask questions.*

WRITING EXERCISE

Bullying isn't limited to kids in school. As adults, we can experience bullying in the workplace, or we could be the ones doing the bullying. Do an assessment of work and personal life.

Are there certain situations or people that make you feel uncomfortable? How would you change it?

_____

_____

_____

_____

_____

_____

_____

_____

_____

_____

_____

_____

DAY 96

February 1, 2018

Addy,

Sometimes the greatest way to say something is to say nothing at all.

Love,
Dad

At some time or another, we've all been told: "If you don't have anything nice to say, then don't say it." It's a simple axiom that is good for each of us to follow. Not everything we think needs to be said. Not everything we think—or say—should be posted on social media.

Silence speaks volumes. Silence can be good or bad. Sometimes our silence says more than our words.

DAY 97

February 2, 2018

Addy,

Friends will come and go like waves in an ocean,
but true friends stay—like a booger in your nose!

Love,
Dad

This note generated the biggest laugh from Addison all school year. *Okay, it was more of a giggle.* I thought I made some great best friends in my first few years of college. I thought it was the circle of friends I'd keep forever. But like waves in an ocean, they came in at high tide, but now they've faded away. They'll come back now and again, and we'll reconnect, but then they're gone again.

My true friends—the ones who were in my wedding, the ones who I check in with on a semiregular basis—have stuck around. Like boogers in my nose that I can't discard.

DAY 98

February 5, 2018

Addy,

Always be ready. Your big moment could be around the corner.

Love,
Dad

Most of my life has been a sports metaphor. Our next opportunity could find us when we least expect it. We should always be ready for what's next.

It may not be possible, but always try to expect the unexpected.

DAY 99

February 6, 2018

Addy,

No matter how many times we argue, or how many times you're mad at me,
You are always number 1 to me. Always.

Love,
Dad

The last few weeks, my and Addison's morning car rides to school haven't been enjoyable. The constant arguing, the constant back talk, the constant poor attitude. It was beginning to become too hard to handle. I was nearing my wit's end with Addison's change in demeanor.

I never want to be mad, upset, or disappointed in my kids. Ever. But now, my disappointment level was climbing. Despite my nearing the peak of anger and disappointment, it was important that reiterate to Addison where I stood. I'll always be her biggest fan and her no. 1 supporter. Nothing will ever change that.

DAY 100

February 7, 2018

Addy,

Some people are like trees, they take *forever* to grow up. And they don't move either.
Don't be a tree!

Love,
Dad

Make like a tree. And leave!

One of my favorite books as a kid and one of my favorite books to read to my kids is *The Giving Tree*. The boy and the tree were best friends, and the tree gave and gave to him until she was a stump. When the boy was an old man, he sat on the stump to rest.

That tree grew up, but she never left the boy's side.

In real life, trees don't move—unless they are swaying in the wind. People move around freely while trees watch us pass them by. Would you rather be the one moving or the one standing still?

DAY 101

February 8, 2018

Addy,

Not everyone will like you. That's okay.
Not everyone likes me.
It's their loss, not ours.

Love,
Dad

If there's one thing I have trouble resolving, it's the fact there are people who don't like me. It's easy for me to tell my daughter *it's their loss, not ours*, but it's not easy for me to believe it.

A terrible workplace environment where bullying was almost encouraged nearly destroyed my psyche. I thought I was strong; I thought I could withstand it. I couldn't. This specific situation led me to seek my first therapist. Little did I know, she would be the first of one, two, three, six.

It took me visiting with my fifth therapist to realize it really was *them*, not me. All this time, I thought I was the one that was broken. I'm still broken, but when people don't like me, it has nothing to do with me. It's a reflection of them.

That's what I want my kids to understand—if someone doesn't like you, that's on them. Not you.

DAY 102

February 19, 2018

Addy,

It's *okay* to dislike someone. But it's *not okay* to disrespect, degrade, and humiliate anyone for any reason. Tell bullies *no.*

Love,
Dad

I started Mardi Gras break with "*It's not you, it's them.*" And I ended the Mardi Gras break with "*It's okay to dislike people, just don't disrespect them.*"

Don't bully people. Don't humiliate others. No matter how much someone may humiliate you, don't reciprocate the action. It may be extremely difficult to follow through, but at least try it.

Today's society and accessibility to technology make it too convenient for us to disrespect, degrade, and humiliate one another. What is there to gain from making ugly remarks from behind your computer screen or your anonymous social media account?

Nothing. Nothing is worth it.

The ends don't—and will never—justify the means.

DAY 103

February 20, 2018

Addy,

Fairy tales are *real*, not because dragons exist, but because dragons *can be beaten*. Solve things like a fairy tale—beat the dragon!

Love,
Dad

Why is it that almost every fairy tale ends with the good guy having to beat the bad guy? There is an obscene amount of fairy tales that feature dragons. Don't tell my son, but dragons aren't real.

When my daughter was four years old, she would always play dress-up in her room, constantly switching her dresses from one fairy-tale princess to another. I almost enjoyed listening to her as she played dress-up and tried to set up tea time and other events for our French Bulldog.

Fairy tales all have a hidden agenda. While they are fictional, they all live in reality. If you think about, fairy tales are real, but dragons are not real. *Sorry, Jack.* But in real life, our foes and our obstacles are dragons. They breathe fear into us; they placate us.

They prove that fairy tales are real, not because dragons are real, but because these dragons—our foes, our fears, our obstacles—can be beaten.

DAY 104

February 21, 2018

Addy,

No matter how much you hate me, dislike me, or yell at me, I'm always here for you. Always.

Love,
Dad

"I love you, but I don't like you right now."

My kids are not always going to like me. I'm dreading the day when Addison will not want anything to do with me. Secretly, I think that's an underlying reason why I write her each morning. I want us to have great daddy-daughter memories before I start being the "uncool" dad. *That would never happen, right?*

As an adult, I went several months without talking to my parents—even going as far as prohibiting them from seeing my kids. It's not the proudest moment of my life. Yet after all this and when I hit rock bottom after losing my job, they were still supporting me and my family.

It's proof as parents that no matter how much we feel like we're failing at this, we'll always be there for our kids. Ashleigh and I will always be there for our kids.

I may not like you right now, but I will always be here for you and I will always love you.

DAY 105

February 22, 2018

Addy,

Your voice can change the world.
Use it. We need it.

Love,
Dad

Social media is a powerful tool, but that doesn't mean you have to be a tool when you use it. Despite the constant intrusion of social media and technology in our lives, they have given us the ability to change the world.

Every day, our voices are changing the world—for better or for worse. Ideally, I'd like my kids' voices to be a positive change for our world. The worst thing we can do is watch the world fly by without using our voice.

Our voice can be silent; our voice can be loud.
Our voice can be good; our voice can be evil.
It's our choice on how we use our voice.
Your voice can change the world; use it.

DAY 106

February 23, 2018

Addy,

Cupcakes have sprinkles. Muffins have wrinkles.
Be a cupcake in a world of muffins!

Love,
Dad

Who doesn't like a bright, colorful, delicious cupcake? Cupcakes are special. They are individually unique. People light up when they see a delicious cupcake. Do those same people light up when they see a muffin? I think not.

Muffins are boring. Cupcakes are not.

Be a cupcake in a world of muffins—*without the frosting, of course.*

DAY 107

February 26, 2018

Addy,

Character is built by being kind, not by being famous.

Love,
Dad

Would you rather be someone everyone wants to get to know or someone who wants to be well-known? Just because you're famous doesn't mean you have great character. Just because you have great character doesn't mean you'll be famous or well-known.

Good character is built by being kind and thinking of others, not by doing the popular thing to gain fame. I don't care about fame. I care about my kids having good character.

Having a good character means you have a good moral compass. It's the compass I want my kids to follow—not a compass led by money or fame. Money and fame are fleeting. Good character—*if you allow it*—will stay with you forever.

DAY 108

February 27, 2018

Addy,

Being different isn't a bad thing. It means you are brave enough to be yourself.

Love,
Dad

Being different is cool. Being different means you're comfortable enough to be yourself and to not follow the pack. I was never brave enough to be myself when I was younger.

I was afraid to be proud of being different. I stayed in the shadows instead. I wasn't brave enough to be myself. I thought being cool *was cool*, not an affront to something else.

I was an awkward preteen, and later I became an awkward teenage. There's a good chance we were *all awkward* at that age, right?

Being cool is *not* different.

Being different is cool. Being different means you're proud of yourself.

DAY 109

February 28, 2018

Addy,

Success is temporary. It's rented. And you must pay the rent every day.

Love,
Dad

Somehow, Addison equated this quote from J. J. Watt as me asking her to pay rent as a nine-year-old. She handed me two quarters, a nickel, a used pencil, and some lint. That's not what I meant.

Success is temporary. It's here one day and overnight—*boom!*—it's gone. Like the bills you pay, you must pay for your success. Bills are due every month, but the rent for your success is due every day.

Climbing the mountain to success is the easy part. The hardest part is staying on top. It's almost as if you have to pay double the rent each day once you reach the top. How do you measure success for a nine-year-old? For me, success for her is building positive habits each day.

Yesterday builds onto today. Today builds onto tomorrow. Tomorrow builds onto the day after tomorrow. Remember, *success is temporary*.

Pay your dues every day (*and don't forget to pay your bills on time*).

WRITING EXERCISE

    As the calendar turns to another year, everyone's minds flock to resolutions. I don't like resolutions. I start each new year with goals: What do I want to do this year? How do I want to get better this year? What goals do you want to start this year?

_____

_____

_____

_____

_____

_____

_____

_____

_____

_____

_____

_____

DAY 110

March 1, 2018

Addy,

Your value doesn't decrease based on someone's inability to see your worth. You're worth $$$.

Love,
Dad

We place too much value on our kids' grades, test scores, or how well they did during the weekend's baseball tournament. Don't let something or someone tell you what you're worth. Your value is priceless.

This past fall, Addison played volleyball for the first time. We signed her up to play because we wanted her to be active, not because we wanted her to be the best outside hitter the recreational sports leagues had ever seen.

During one of her first games, I overheard some parents discussing the possibility of their daughters getting college scholarships to play volleyball. This upset me because these parents were already connecting their kids' athletic abilities to the value of a college education. That's not fair.

When we put that type of value on someone, we are disappointed when they don't reach the heights we expect. Our kids are worth it, but we can't put a price tag on them.

DAY 111

March 2, 2018

Addy,

Be who you are and say what you feel because those who mind *don't matter* and those who matter *don't mind*.

Love,
Dad

It's Dr. Seuss's birthday. I mean, who doesn't love Dr. Seuss?

DAY 112

March 5, 2018

Hello, Addy,

Good morning! Have a great, ridiculously amazing day!

Love,
Dad

Nothing witty, nothing gained. Wrong.

Why not tell her to have a great, ridiculously amazing day to shake things up?

No one else determines our mood for the day except us. We determine whether or not we have a great, ridiculously amazing day.

DAY 113

March 6, 2018

Addy,

We're not defined by how many times we get knocked down. We're defined by how many times we get back up.

Love,
Dad

We all love a good story. What's better than a good story? A comeback story. We're all writing a comeback story. We are all coming back from something.

If you get knocked down eight times, then you need to get up nine times. We're always getting knocked down by others. It's painful to get back up at times, but we have to dust ourselves off and try it again.

Which story line would you rather want—you got knocked down and didn't get up, or you got knocked down and got up again?

Get back up.

DAY 114

March 7, 2018

Addy,

Those who are mean to you need your kindness the most.

Love,
Dad

Those who are mean to us need us. Turn the other cheek. Don't let them see the pain they've caused. Those who are mean to you are missing kindness in their life.

Fill that void with kindness not with hate. Fill that void with an act of kindness without any expectation of something in return. It took me a long time to understand that those who mistreated me were upset about something in their lives. They projected that void onto me.

Project kindness on those projecting anger.

DAY 115

March 8, 2018

Addy,

Most people won't notice your hard work or when you do good things. Don't chase others' approval. Only chase your own.

Love,
Dad

In hindsight, most of self-esteem issues centered around where I placed that energy—at work. I gauged my self-esteem and self-worth on what I accomplished at work and the number of pats on the back. I was chasing the approval of my bosses and my coworkers. My first promotion was based on the hard work and the quality of the results I produced.

Consequently, I paid a price for it. Yeah, I got the promotion I had desired, and a nice pay raise to support my family that was about to grow to four. But I paid for it with my self-esteem taking a dramatic free fall. I endured harassment and workplace bullying by some of my coworkers. My depression worsened; I stopped caring about my appearance and my health.

I chase others' approval, and I got burned. It wasn't until seven years and a second career later when I realized that none of that matters. The only approval that matters is your own. I don't put my name on anything that I'm not proud of.

Stop chasing other people. Focus on the tasks at hand and focus on making yourself happy.

DAY 116

March 12, 2018

Addy,

When life gives you Monday, dip it in glitter and make it sparkle all day.

Love,
Dad

Admit it—we all have suffered a case of the Mondays, but I didn't think my analogy of "If life gives you lemons, then pour vodka in a glass and make adult lemonade" would have been appropriate for my nine-year-old. Mondays don't wake up and decide to make our lives miserable. We are the ones that wake up and decide to make our Mondays miserable.

Instead of waking up with the assumption that your Monday will suck, wake up, tell Monday to put its glitter paint on, and rock it. Glitter makes everything better except when you have to clean it up.

DAY 117

March 13, 2018

Addy,

It's better to be *strong* than pretty and useless.

Love,
Dad

Women are not arm candy. They aren't here for us to gawk. My daughter is too smart, too witty, and too talented to sit around for someone's amusement. I want her to be strong and outspoken. That's prettier to me than someone who is naturally pretty but offers nothing.

Teach your daughter to be strong and to stand up for herself. If I wanted something pretty and useless, then I'd buy a plant.

DAY 118

March 14, 2018

Addy,

If you aren't willing to work for it, don't complain about not having it.

Love,
Dad

We live in the era of participation trophies. No one is willing to work for anything anymore. We expect things to be magically handed to us because we asked or because we think we deserved it. That's not how this works.

Put in the work. If you put in the work and don't have something, then you have the right to complain about not having it. If you aren't willing to put in the blood, sweat, and tears, then you forfeit your right to complain about not having something you want.

If you *really* want something, then you are going to do whatever it takes to get it. People are going to remember you for what you do or didn't do, not what you complained about not having.

DAY 119

March 15, 2018

Addy,

Look at your feet.
Look at the stars.
Anything is possible if you dream and make it happen.

Love,
Dad

Addison read this during our morning drive to school. Since she was in the car; she only saw the roof of the car when she looked up.

"This doesn't make sense, Daddy."

"It will make sense once you're outside and look up."

She gave me an exaggerated eye roll. This is my surprised look.

My point this morning was *supposed to be this*: The sky is the limit, and we are able to do anything we set our mind to. As long as our feet are moving, we can reach for the stars and achieve our dreams.

I want my kids to keep moving. You can't accomplish anything if you're standing still.

DAY 120

March 16, 2018

Addy,

Beauty isn't about having a pretty face. It's about having a pretty mind, a pretty heart, and a pretty soul.

Love,
Dad

I'm no Brad Pitt. I don't turn women's heads when I enter a room, but I so desperately try to be a good person with a pretty mind, a pretty heart, and a somewhat pretty soul. Our society focuses too much on beauty. And while I think my daughter is beautiful, there will be people who don't or who will judge her solely on her exterior appearance.

I want her to grow up knowing that beauty is what's inside despite what all the glamour magazines tell us.

Your exterior attractiveness may open doors for you, but your interior attractiveness (mind, heart, and soul) is what people will want to know about you.

DAY 121

March 19, 2018

Addy,

Believe in something so much that you don't give up. People will try to knock you down. Stand up and change the world anyway.

Love,
Dad

We all have our different beliefs. Some of us have stronger beliefs than others. Some of us tend to drop our beliefs when people question us or don't agree with us. Why are we so quick to abandon our beliefs?

I don't want—or expect—people to believe the same things I believe. This may sound weird, but I want people to disagree with me. I enjoy disagreements because I can learn more about someone's side of the argument. It's hard for others to knock me down with things I firmly believe in. I'm not sure that's a positive attribute of mine or not.

Whatever your beliefs, whatever your thoughts, don't let anyone try to knock you down. If you truly believe, then stand up for those beliefs. Push the critics aside and change the world anyway.

DAY 122

March 20, 2018

Addy,

You are good enough. Remember that.

Love,
Dad

Sometimes, we all need a bit of affirmation. This morning, I felt that Addison was in need of some affirmation.

Sometimes, all we want to know is that everything is okay and that everything is going to be okay.

That is enough.

DAY 123

March 26, 2018

Addy,

Be nice to people on the way up in life because you may meet them again on the way down.

Love,
Dad

Imagine life as a ladder. Each rung is a different stage of your life or your career. As you climb each rung, you are inevitably passing someone else. When you pass others, do you kindly wave at them and say *"Hi,"* or do you scowl and push them down as you push yourself up?

In the moment, it may seem like we'll never see those people or never work with them again, but as big as the world is, it is a small world. Why use people for your personal gain? It may feel good at first, but it'll hurt you in the long run.

Use money and love people; don't love money and use people.

DAY 124

March 27, 2018

Addy,

We can control only two things in life:
1. Our attitude every day
2. How we respond to situations
It's on *us*.

Love,
Dad

Everything is on *us*.

No one else controls our attitude or how we respond to situations. Other people may upset us or do something that puts us in a precarious situation, but we are the ones that determine the outcome.

What people do to us is a reflection of them, not us. How we act every day and the attitude we choose are on *us*. Choose your attitude and how you respond to others.

It's on you; it's on me. It's on us.

DAY 125

March 28, 2018

Addy,

We make our *choices*. Then, our choices *make us*.

Love,
Dad

If this, then that. If that, then this.

Whether consciously or subconsciously, we make choices. Each choice compounds on another choice and another and another. Our choices are like the bricks used to build a house. Each brick has a value. With every choice we make, another brick is laid.

Brick by brick, our choices ultimately build us. We are the product of our decisions. As much as we want to point fingers, we cannot blame others for our situation except ourselves. Your boss didn't force you to lose your job. Your neighbor didn't cause you to file for bankruptcy. Your dog didn't ask you to go on a Target shopping spree and spend all your rent money.

We make our choices, and our choices make us.

DAY 126

March 29, 2018

Addy,

We are all "weird." There is no such thing as "normal." When someone calls you weird, say thank you.

Love,
Dad

Who decided that "normal" is the baseline for everything? Who is the one to define what "normal" is? In either case, "normal" doesn't exist.

We should celebrate our weirdness. Nothing we do is *normal*. If we were all to be considered normal, then each day would be rather mundane and boring. Each of us are unique in our own weird ways.

Being weird is a good thing. When someone calls you weird, take it as the utmost compliment. Say thank you.

WRITING EXERCISE

Spring is as good of a time as any to do some "spring cleaning" and assess your new year goals. Review your goals from earlier. Did you accomplish what you set out to accomplish: Why or why not? What could you have done differently? What did you learn?

_____

_____

_____

_____

_____

_____

_____

_____

_____

_____

_____

_____

_____

DAY 127

April 9, 2018

Addy,

If you're not learning, then you're not living.
Always. Be. Learning.

Love,
Dad

Want to have a successful day? Learn something new.

We all stand to learn something new each day. We cannot realistically make ourselves or those around us better if we aren't learning something new.

I went back to school to pursue a PhD, not because I wanted to become Dr. Yandle, but to make myself better. I want to be a lifelong learner. Granted, making myself better is also simultaneously making me poorer, but it'll all be worth it in the end.

Make yourself better.

DAY 128

April 10, 2018

Addy,

Don't remind people how smart you are. Show them with your actions, not your words.

Love,
Dad

People that feel the need to tell people how smart they are cannot truly be as smart as they think. We shouldn't waste our energy on telling others how smart we are. Is it worth it? Is it necessary?

In the real world, no one cares about your GPA in college. No one cares about your test scores.

Show people how smart you are with your actions. Show them what you can by doing it, not by saying it.

DAY 129

April 11, 2018

Addy,

Eat glitter for breakfast and *shine* all day!

Love,
Dad

Man, that guy eats *nails* for breakfast! Why would anyone want to eat nails for breakfast? Really? My daughter gets her nails painted and eats glitter for breakfast. *Boom*. I win!

There was really no point to this day's note except to see my daughter's smile shine brightly that day.

And to try my hand at drawing glitter.

DAY 130

April 16, 2018

Addy,

No one has changed the world by standing still.
Keep moving.

Love,
Dad

Dogs don't bark at parked cars. It took me a ridiculously long time to figure out what this saying meant. I did have to explain to Addison what it meant, but it made sense to her after I explained it.

Don't stand still.

When we stand still, other people pass us by. We fall farther and farther behind while others keep moving.

Want to change the world? Keep doing what you're doing.

DAY 131

April 17, 2018

Addy,

Make sure the choices you make are worth the losses you'll take.

Love,
Dad

Choices lead to consequences. Our choices determine the life we have. Our choices are like investments. Every investment—good or bad—leads to a result. If we make a good investment, then we reap the benefits. If we make a bad investment, then we'll lose money. When we make investments, we're uncertain whether or not it's a good choice or a bad choice.

Before we complete a decision transaction, we need to first be okay with the outcome. A risk-taker or not, we must take the good with the bad.

DAY 132

April 18, 2018

Addy,

Pobody's nerfect. We all make misteaks.

Love,
Dad

Another perfectly written joke note, another perfectly executed joke fail.

A perfectly cooked steak is delicious, but a perfectly cooked misteak is not. The fact of the matter is, nobody's perfect.

Make a mistake? Own it. Mistakes make us human and more endearing to others. We don't want to surround ourselves with people who don't make mistakes or who aren't willing to admit they were wrong.

Pobody's nerfect. Accept them; accept yourself.

DAY 133

April 19, 2018

Addy,

Bad habits are like a comfy bed—really easy to get into and really hard to get out of.

Love,
Dad

I have bad habits I've been trying to break for thirty-five years, but they are just so comfy! We all have bad habits. Bad habits are comfortable, and we are creatures of habit and comfort.

We want to stay in our comfort zone. It means we don't have to change. Or we've convinced ourselves we don't have to change.

As comfortable as the bed is, we must roll out of it every morning.

DAY 134

April 20, 2018

Addy,

Your smile brightens my cloudiest days.

Love,
Dad

I don't smile nearly as often—mainly because I'm self-conscious about my semidouble chins when I do. I love seeing my kids happy and carefree. When I have a bad day, my kids make it better, except when they are screaming at each other or driving their mother nuts.

I remember when Addison was a baby and her face would light up when I'd come home from work. Jackson was the same way when he was little. I always loved when they'd run to the door when I'd come home from a long road trip.

They always brighten my cloudiest days.

DAY 135

April 23, 2018

Addy,

If you're the smartest person in the room, then you're in the wrong room.

Love,
Dad

Every time I tweet this quote, the general response is: *"But what if someone else is the smartest person in the room, do they have to leave? Then the next smartest person would have to leave too, right?"*

The quote is not literal. It's a reminder that we are all a work in progress.

I'm not the smartest person in the room. You're not the smartest person in the room. I'm not the smartest person in this book! If you have to tell people how smart you are, then you aren't willing to learn from others.

DAY 136

April 24, 2018

Addy,

Do as I say, not necessarily as I do. I've made mistakes in my life, but I've learned from them.

Love,
Dad

Before the dawn of Twitter, I said a lot of things. Since the dawn of Twitter, I have said a much-larger number of things—most of which make sense. Some of things I've said make no sense at all. Despite my small habit of saying nonsensical things, much of what I do say—I think—carries value. The things I do say are better than some of the things I do.

While people remember what you do and how you made them feel, I want my kids to do as I say, not as I do. Some of my actions are bad habits, but I've learned from those mistakes.

Watch your words; they become actions.

Watch your actions; you become them.

Do as I say, not necessarily as I do.

DAY 137

April 25, 2018

Addy,

Never judge a book by its cover. Always read the pages before you decide.

Love,
Dad

Too many people only read the *Yelp!* reviews or the critics' quotes on the back of a book. Don't let other peoples' views decide what you think. Everyone has different tastes.

If our friends like something, that doesn't mean we will like it too. Liking something or disliking something is completely subjective. We all have varying opinions on what we think is good.

Don't always take others' subjective opinions for your own. Take the time to figure out if you like it.

Always read the story. Everyone's story is worth reading.

DAY 138

April 26, 2018

Addy,

Learn to accept the word *no*. *No* is not an end to something. It's a beginning to something else.

Love,
Dad

I hear *no* multiple times every year.

No is not an end to something. It's a beginning to something else.

When someone tells you *no*, you accept their decision and move on. Just because that door closed doesn't mean all the doors are closed to other things. Too many of us get mad and unnerved when we hear the word *no*.

Accept it and move on.

DAY 139

April 27, 2018

Addy,

Everyone is replaceable. Make yourself unforgettable.

Love,
Dad

No, I'm not threatening to replace my nine-year-old daughter. My kids are not replaceable. They do make themselves unforgettable. I mean, our house hasn't been quiet in ten years.

Our friends will replace us with someone cooler or someone who has more similar interests, likes, or dislikes. We will always be replaced in something. But did we make ourselves unforgettable? Make people remember what you did for them.

We're all replaceable in our jobs, but we all have the chance to make ourselves unforgettable.

DAY 140

April 30, 2018

Addy,

You are more than any test score. Whatever you do, I'll love you just the same. Good luck! Breathe!

Love,
Dad

Today marked the first day of weeklong state standardized testing for the fourth grade at her school. My daughter was riddled with anxiety, but I wanted to keep her calm. Standardized testing can be stressful, and we wanted her to know that she is more than a test score.

She might be a test score to the state, but she's a sweet, loving, and funny nine-year-old girl to us.

WRITING EXERCISE

Standardized tests make me anxious. They make my kids anxious. Addison's teachers asked parents to write notes to their kids each day during the week of state testing. What would you write to your kids as they prepare for important tests or projects at school?

_____

_____

_____

_____

_____

_____

_____

_____

_____

_____

_____

_____

DAY 141

May 1, 2018

Addy,

Your value doesn't decrease based on someone's (or some test's) inability to see your worth.

Love,
Dad

No person or test should ever dictate your value to others or how you measure your self-worth. Whether we realize it or not, we put an immense amount of stress and pressure on our kids to perform academically. Annoying youth sports parents put a ridiculous amount of stress on their kids to become the next Bo Jackson or Michael Jordan. Last time I checked, there are no college recruiters scouting coach-pitch baseball.

The point is, don't let others tell you what you're worth. I'll view my children the same, whether they score a perfect score on the SAT or if they score the lowest in their class. Their value won't increase or decrease with their score. They are still worth the same no matter what they do.

Priceless.

DAY 142

May 2, 2018

Addy,

You become what you believe. I believe in *you*.

Love,
Dad

You become what you believe. You believe what you've become.

It's like a vision board. If you believe that you can become something, then you have the power within yourself to possibly make it happen. Addison, for the most part, believes she is a smart and creative nine-year-old.

I will support whatever my kids believe and want to become. I didn't always have support in my initial career choice, and I didn't have great support when I decided to give up on my career to try something else.

All you need to do is believe in something, and someone will believe in you.

DAY 143

May 3, 2018

Addy,

You solve problems with *solutions*, not *excuses*.

Love,
Dad

Making excuses is the easy way out. We can all complain about problems or the decisions we don't like. Do we offer solutions to those complaints?

As a leader, I always prodded my staff with my desire for them to present ideas and solutions, not simple complaints about what they didn't like. I take the same stance with my kids.

"Daddy, Jack hit me!"

"Daddy, Addy won't leave me alone!"

Don't complain about the things going on. Offer possible solutions to prevent situations from happening again. It's human nature for us not to offer possible solutions when we make excuses.

Next time you are ready to complain about something or make an excuse why something did or didn't happen, provide a solution instead.

DAY 144

May 4, 2018

Addy,

My two favorite F-words are *finish Friday*. Finish strong!

Love,
Dad

Addison seriously thought I was going to write something else.
I almost wrote "French fries."
It is apparent, I probably should wash my mouth out with soap.

DAY 145

May 7, 2018

Addy,

A bad attitude is like a flat tire—you won't go anywhere until you change it.

Love,
Dad

We can't drive a car with a flat tire. We must change it. Whether you change the flat tire yourself or your mechanic does it, we can't drive our car until we get it done.

A flat tire is like a bad attitude. It's not going to change unless we do something about it. We can't depend on others to change our bad attitude. We are responsible for changing it.

Don't let the "disease of me" control you.

DAY 146

May 8, 2018

Addy,

Compliments are like tissues, except we shouldn't
be so quick to throw them away.
Keep them.

Love,
Dad

People offer you a tissue. You say thank you. We blow our nose, and then we throw it away. But you don't wad these up and them away. Compliments aren't always easily dispensable.

I'm not very good at accepting compliments. It's seldom that I believe people when they give me a compliment. It has nothing to do with them; it has everything to do with me. It's hard for me to accept compliments. When I sneeze, I will always take a tissue.

When I blow my nose into the tissue, I promptly throw it away. When I *finally* accept a compliment, I accept it and try to remember it. Those are the kind of tissues I want to keep, not the ones full of boogers.

A pocket full of compliments is great. A pocket full of booger-filled tissues, not so much.

DAY 147

May 9, 2018

Addy,

It isn't what we say or think that defines us but what we do.

Love,
Dad

People will forget the things you say, but they'll always remember the things you do. As a kid, I have forgotten most of what my parents said to me. There isn't much I remember from things my teachers or professors said in school. But I do remember how they made me feel.

When I was a senior in high school, my honors English teacher called me up to the blackboard, and he asked me to fix the grammar on one of our homework questions.

I was wrong. *Strike 1.*

He asked me again. I was wrong, again. *Strike 2.*

Three more times he asked me, and three more times I was wrong. *Strikes 3, 4, and 5.*

After the fifth wrong answer, he walked over to the window and asked me, "Do you see any flying jackasses outside?"

"No, sir, I don't."

"That's right because the only jackass I see is you."

Since then, I vowed that no one would ever embarrass me like that again, and I would become a grammar snob.

DAY 148

May 10, 2018

Addy,

Everyone you meet has something to teach you.

Love,
Dad

We are all teachers. We aren't walking around teaching random people calculus or physics or Latin, but we're teaching something to everyone we meet. Maybe it's how to tie a tie. Maybe it's how to get your timing down for the perfect joke.

Maybe it's how to start the book-writing process.

Whatever it is, we are teaching something to someone. We are learning something from someone else. We don't know everything. We are lifelong learners.

Teach something. Learn something.

DAY 149

May 11, 2018

Addy,

If you're early, you're on time. If you're on time, you're late. If you're late, you're forgotten.

Love,
Dad

Our high school baseball coach was always a stickler for us being on time. It was the first day of my freshman year of high school—a new school and I feel like I'm drowning from the stress. I'm lost on campus, and I'm already late for second-period PE.

I finally find the right entrance to the gym, race up the stairs, and run onto the basketball court. I can't talk because I'm panting so hard.

"Hey! You know what time second period starts?"

I nod a faint yes as I'm still catching my breath.

"If you're early, you're on time. If you're on time, you're late. You're late."

To be fair, I wasn't on time. I was late—at least five minutes late. I thought I stumbled into a philosophy class, not PE.

His words have stuck with me for the last twenty-plus years.

DAY 150

May 14, 2018

Addy,

A mistake repeated more than once is a decision.
Be careful with your decisions.

Love,
Dad

We are what we repeatedly do. One mistake is an accident. The same mistake multiple times is called a decision. I make mistakes all the time. I *try* to avoid making the same mistakes again. Of course, as I learned throughout the course of this book, I am a creature of habit.

I tend to write similar things over and over again. I tend to make the same decision over and over again. Thus, I tend to make the same mistake over and over again.

These are all my decisions. I make a conscious effort to fight my subconscious with well-thought decisions. As a creature of habit, sometimes our mistakes and our decisions are on autopilot.

Be careful with your decisions.

DAY 151

May 15, 2018

Addy,

No one cares how much you know until they know how much you care.

Love,
Dad

And many people don't care how much you know at all.

I learned this as a manager. I could have all the right answers to my staff's questions, but if they don't know I care about them as individuals, then I am just a talking head. None of us should ever work in the "knowledge" business. We should all concentrate on working in the "people" business.

That starts as kids. You can have the perfect grades, the perfect tests, and the greatest essay for college applications, but what do you have to show for it? I'd rather have my kids get straight Cs in school but be active in civic organizations and give back to their community than get straight As but not be involved with bettering other people.

What you know will get you jobs and opportunities, but how you treat people and how you connect with them will help you keep those jobs and opportunities.

DAY 152

May 16, 2018

Addy,

It takes zero effort to be mean to others. It takes hard work and effort to be humble and kind to others.
Do the work!

Love,
Dad

Being mean and disrespectful to others takes no effort. It's too easy to be ugly to people in today's world. Use your time wisely and just be nice to other people!

No one wants to do the work anymore. It's now, now, now! That's why when someone doesn't get our order right or we don't get a grade we "think" we deserve, we unleash into a profanity-filled tirade. That's the easiest thing to do.

Take the few extra minutes to figure out *why* we didn't get what we wanted or what we thought we deserved. Taking the easy way, the road most traveled, is a cop-out. Take the road less traveled, the road that takes the most effort to navigate, the road without a map.

Discover things, figure them out on your own. There's no roadmap to be kind to others, but there always appears to be a roadmap to being mean to other people.

While I don't support profanity-laced tirades, let that be your absolute, absolute, absolute last resort (see also: never).

DAY 153

May 17, 2018

Addy,

Nothing is *impossible*. Tell yourself, "I'm possible."

Love,
Dad

Nothing is too hard to understand or accomplish. Yes, it may be difficult at first, but when you put in the time, it will pay off. I don't want Addison shying away from things because she thinks they are "too hard."

Challenge yourself. Prove it to yourself you can overcome any obstacle. In hindsight, I think that's why I kept getting up every morning after I lost my job and was unsuccessfully searching for a new one. I wanted to prove it to myself that I could overcome anything.

Fourth grade is challenging, but it's easy to conquer. And you know what? Fifth grade will be more challenging, but you will conquer that too. Each year will continue to get more and more challenging, but after a while, you'll gain the tools you need to conquer it.

DAY 154

May 18, 2018

Addy,

Life isn't rainbows and unicorns. It can be hard.
It's *okay* to have a bad day.

Love,
Dad

Sometimes, I think I'm moodier as an adult than I was as a teenager. On this particular Friday morning, it wasn't 6:00 a.m., and I was *already* in a bad mood. My mind was preoccupied with a list of thoughts, but I knew how today was going to end—worse than it started.

Suffering from depression means that some days will be better than others. This was one of those "other" days. I'm sure my parenting style won't sit well with others, but I'd rather my kids see me suffering from bad days instead of hiding behind a false facade of smiles, sunshine, and rainbows.

That's not life. I still have yet to see a real-life unicorn. I want my kids to know that we all have bad days and that we still have to get up and get through the day. That's real life. Addison has had bad days. I have bad days.

Life isn't rainbows and unicorns.

DAY 155

May 21, 2018

Addy,

Happiness is not a fish you can catch. If it were, then we'd be happier and less hungry for more.

Love,
Dad

We catch balls and colds. We cannot catch happiness. If it were as easy as baiting a hook and dropping a line in the water, then more people would be happy. Unfortunately, happiness isn't a fish in a lake or an ocean.

We make our own happiness. We make our circumstances. We adapt our lives to our decisions. There were times in my life when I wish happiness was a fish I could catch because I craved instant gratification, but that's not how it works.

Happiness is not a fish you can catch.

DAY 156

May 22, 2018

Addy,

The truth doesn't cost you anything. But a lie could cost you everything.

Love,
Dad

Lying is never worth it. Sure, it might make your friend feel better (when they don't realize you are sparing their feelings), or it gets you out of trouble for the time being. But every lie comes with a price.

You may not pay that price right away. You may have to pay for it later, and many times, *later* means paying for it with another lie and another and another. I'm not an economics guy, but I think that's compound interest or something like that? Either way, lies have cost people their jobs, their marriages, their reputation.

To me, no lie is worth losing my job, my family or damaging my reputation and character that I have worked so hard to build—the right way. Don't build your life in a house of lies. Like a deck of cards, it'll all come crashing down with a gentle breeze.

DAY 157

May 23, 2018

Addy,

Finish the school year the same way you started it—*with a smile and a great attitude!*

Love,
Dad

That sound you hear? That's the sound Ashleigh makes when she realizes that school is over and summer is here. Today, my daughter leaves the house as a fourth grader and comes home as a fifth grader.

She started the school year with a big smile and a great attitude, and I wanted her to finish the year the same way. I want her to end each school year with good memories. I know one thing for sure: she has a helluva lot more confidence at the end of fourth grade than she did when she started.

I'll celebrate that small victory.

AFTERWORD

I've always enjoyed writing. Some of my teachers over the years said I had a talent for it. I've always viewed writing as a therapeutic exercise where I didn't have to talk—I just let my words do the talking for me. As an introvert, it can be exhausting and/or scary as hell for me to share my feelings and my emotions aloud. I don't emote often. Writing down my thoughts and feelings or expressing myself through written words has always been my preferred method of communication.

Writing makes me feel safe. As weird—or as sweet—as it may seem, writing notes to my daughter is easier for me than giving her advice verbally. Don't get me wrong—I still talk to my daughter. It's not like we're only texting each other or sending smoke signals. We talk every morning on our way to school. It's something I look forward to each morning. It may only be a three-minute drive to her school, but at least we have some time together to talk or for me to tell a ridiculously horrible joke or for her to vent about school or her brother or her dog.

One of my dreams was to write a book. I've entertained a myriad of ideas (in my head, of course) about a book to pen, but I would get dejected within moments of putting keys to keyboard and I'd scrap it. This book, this book you are reading now, was the suggestion of my daughter's middle school principal.

During the course of the school year, I posted my notes on Twitter, Facebook, and Instagram. The feedback I received from the few moments of selflessness I take each day for my daughter was overwhelming positive and refreshing. Some of my notes resonated with people more than others. A few months into the school year, Addison's teacher contacted me to ask permission to share some of the notes with the class. Her principal said reading the notes on Facebook was the highlight of her day.

But while those on the receiving end of my social media posts saw the messages I wrote, they did not see the full scope of what was going on in our house.

Fourth grade is tough for any kid, particularly girls. Middle school girls can be mean and hurtful. It's all part of growing up, but it's not fun as a parent to witness your child being hurt on a daily basis. While my daily #DadLunchNotes may give the impression that I am a perfect father and my daughter is soaking up my advice like a sponge, both couldn't be further from reality.

In reality, my daughter and I are 99 percent alike, according to my wife (I think it's more seventy-thirty, but whatever). We are so much alike that we are constantly butting heads like two rams backing up and running full speed at the other. *Bam!* We lock horns, and then we go back at it. We are both headstrong and stubborn, but I see me in Addison. I don't want Addison to endure what I endured as a kid. I want her to be a strong, vocal, and resilient woman.

Up until the start of fourth grade, Addison hadn't had any problems at school. She was a happy kid with a great attitude. When her attitude shifted midway through the school year, my wife and I chalked it up to puberty and the hormonal changes that overwhelm kids at this age. We soon learned, however, that it wasn't hormones.

Addison became moody, resistant, isolated, anxious, impatient.

At first, we didn't understand why. We thought she was getting a head start on her teenage years. There was plenty of yelling, plenty of crying, plenty of punishments handed down.

I'm not proud of the yelling. I hate seeing my daughter cry. It was devastating to see her hurt and not have a solution. Here I was, writing notes in the morning, notes I *thought* were helping my daughter on some level, but they weren't. I was missing the mark.

She eventually told us why: she was being bullied at school. My wife and I were bullied as kids in private school, which is probably why we are both jaded about private school education.

The bullying took a toll on Addison mentally and understandably so. She takes things personally. I take things personally. We all take things personally. It's hard not to.

Not only was Addison acting out because she was being bullied; we soon learned she would be diagnosed with ADHD—attention deficit hyperactivity disorder. It was all starting to make more sense now. Hindsight is always twenty-twenty, and I was upset at myself for missing the signs earlier.

As the school year was winding down, things got better. The storm had finally passed, and the clouds were beginning to break as the sun began to return.

* * * * *

A year of writing these notes, and I learned more about my daughter and maybe even more about myself. I learned I'm not a perfect parent; I will never be a perfect parent. Rather, I'm perfectly imperfect.

Chris

AFTERWORD

(These are actual words written by an actual nine-year-old.)

Okay, so I learned that people aren't perfect. We should be nice to every person even if nobody is watching.

[These notes] made me feel uplifted. Here is the definition of *uplifted*—"Elevate or stimulate (someone) morally or spiritually." I found this definition on Google.

My favorite parts were during the holidays because they told me a good lesson or a joke that teaches a lesson!

XOXO,
Addison

WRITING PROMPTS

This section includes writing prompts and writing activities for parents (dads, specifically) and kids to begin writing notes. Not everyone is fortunate enough to have writing come so naturally. For some people, writing is an excruciating and exhausting practice. For others like me, it can be therapeutic and cathartic.

My hope is the following pages will ease your writing anxiety and help you cultivate your creativity. We don't want our kids to be perfect; we want them to try. We don't want our parents to be perfect; we just want them to be with us.

PARENT WRITING PROMPTS

Writing Prompt No. 1

What motivates you?

_____

_____

_____

_____

_____

_____

_____

_____

_____

_____

_____

_____

_____

PARENT WRITING PROMPTS

Writing Prompt No. 2

What makes your child smile?

_____

_____

_____

_____

_____

_____

_____

_____

_____

_____

_____

_____

_____

_____

PARENT WRITING PROMPTS

Writing Prompt No. 3

How does your child inspire you to be a better father or mother?

_____

_____

_____

_____

_____

_____

_____

_____

_____

_____

_____

_____

PARENT WRITING PROMPTS

Writing Prompt No. 4

What do you wish you could do better as a dad or mom?

_____

_____

_____

_____

_____

_____

_____

_____

_____

_____

_____

_____

_____

PARENT WRITING PROMPTS

Writing Prompt No. 5

How can small gestures like writing notes help make your child's day better?

_____

_____

_____

_____

_____

_____

_____

_____

_____

_____

_____

_____

_____

PARENT WRITING PROMPTS

Writing Prompt No. 6

Write an encouraging note that you wish you received when you were your child's age.

_____

_____

_____

_____

_____

_____

_____

_____

_____

_____

_____

_____

PARENT WRITING PROMPTS

Writing Prompt No. 7

Tell your child: my favorite part of the day was when I was with you and we _____.

_____

_____

_____

_____

_____

_____

_____

_____

_____

_____

_____

PARENT WRITING PROMPTS

Writing Prompt No. 8

Tell your kids about the day they were born and how you felt when you held them for the first time.

_____

_____

_____

_____

_____

_____

_____

_____

_____

_____

_____

_____

_____

PARENT WRITING PROMPTS

Writing Prompt No. 9

Our children are faced with more stress than we did as kids. Tell them how you overcome fear and how that can help them cope with their own fears.

_____

_____

_____

_____

_____

_____

_____

_____

_____

_____

_____

_____

PARENT WRITING PROMPTS

Writing Prompt No. 10

Thanks to social media, we only see everyone's "perfect" lives, but we know our lives are far from perfect. How would you tell your kids about the challenges of trying to be perfect?

_____

_____

_____

_____

_____

_____

_____

_____

_____

_____

_____

_____

KID WRITING PROMPTS

Writing Prompt No. 1

What motivates you?

_____

_____

_____

_____

_____

_____

_____

_____

_____

_____

_____

_____

_____

_____

KID WRITING PROMPTS

Writing Prompt No. 2

How does your mom and dad make you smile?

_____

_____

_____

_____

_____

_____

_____

_____

_____

_____

_____

_____

KID WRITING PROMPTS

Writing Prompt No. 3

Who inspires you and why?

_____

_____

_____

_____

_____

_____

_____

_____

_____

_____

_____

_____

KID WRITING PROMPTS

Writing Prompt No. 4

Pick three new things you want to learn and what you can do with them.

_____

_____

_____

_____

_____

_____

_____

_____

_____

_____

_____

_____

_____

_____

KID WRITING PROMPTS

Writing Prompt No. 5

How can small gestures like writing notes help another person's day better?

_____

_____

_____

_____

_____

_____

_____

_____

_____

_____

_____

_____

KID WRITING PROMPTS

Writing Prompt No. 6

Write a classmate an encouraging note that would make you feel better.

_____

_____

_____

_____

_____

_____

_____

_____

_____

_____

_____

_____

_____

KID WRITING PROMPTS

Writing Prompt No. 7

Tell your mom and dad: my favorite part of the day was when I was with you and we _____.

_____

_____

_____

_____

_____

_____

_____

_____

_____

_____

_____

KID WRITING PROMPTS

Writing Prompt No. 8

Write a short story about an adventure you had with your friend.

_____

_____

_____

_____

_____

_____

_____

_____

_____

_____

_____

_____

KID WRITING PROMPTS

Writing Prompt No. 9

What do you want to be when you grow up? Why? What can you do
to make it happen?

_____

_____

_____

_____

_____

_____

_____

_____

_____

_____

_____

_____

KID WRITING PROMPTS

Writing Prompt No. 10

How can you use your social media accounts for social good?

_____

_____

_____

_____

_____

_____

_____

_____

_____

_____

_____

_____

NOTE PAGES

We all need help on where to start. Here are some example notes to help you begin this journey with your child.

> *(Child's name),*
> *I love you more than any other human being on Earth.*
>
> *Love,*
> *Dad*

What else would you say or would you add? Write your own below.

_____

_____

_____

_____

_____

_____

_____

_____

_____

NOTE PAGES

(Child's name),
The world needs more leaders, not more followers.
Be a leader.

Love,
Dad

What else would you say or would you add? Write your own below.

_____

_____

_____

_____

_____

_____

_____

_____

_____

_____

NOTE PAGES

(Child's name),
Make a new friend today.

Love,
Dad

What else would you say or would you add? Write your own below.

_____

_____

_____

_____

_____

_____

_____

_____

_____

NOTE PAGES

(Child's name),
Always find something that makes you happy.

Love,
Dad

What else would you say or would you add? Write your own below.

_____

_____

_____

_____

_____

_____

_____

_____

_____

_____

NOTE PAGES

(Child's name),
The only thing brighter than the sun is your smile!

Love,
Dad

What else would you say or would you add? Write your own below.

_____

_____

_____

_____

_____

_____

_____

_____

_____

_____

NOTE PAGES

(Child's name),
No one said life was going to be easy. It's not how many times you get knocked down but how many times you get back up.

Love,
Dad

What else would you say or would you add? Write your own below.

_____

_____

_____

_____

_____

_____

_____

_____

_____

NOTE PAGES

(Child's name),
You waste more energy being angry than being
happy. Be happy.

Love,
Dad

What else would you say or would you add? Write your own below.

_____

_____

_____

_____

_____

_____

_____

_____

_____

ABOUT THE AUTHOR

Chris Yandle is a former college athletics public relations professional who has fully transitioned to a career in academia. He has dedicated his professional career to education and being a bright example for his kids. A previously published college textbook author, he is an adjunct college instructor and is currently working research for his PhD. Chris and his wife, Ashleigh, live in Mandeville, Louisiana, with their children Addison and Jackson, and their dogs Tank and Benson. You can find Chris on Twitter at @chrisyandle.

CPSIA information can be obtained
at www.ICGtesting.com
Printed in the USA
BVHW081116010721
610975BV00006B/238

9 781643 507354